JUST A

TEACHER

JUST A TEACHER

Trailer Park Tales and Backwoods Lore

DAVID TOURZAN

ELLAQUENT PRESS
Just a Teacher: Trailer Park Tales and Backwoods Lore
David Tourzan

Copyright©2015 by David Tourzan
Copyeditor: Friends and Family
Cover Design: David Tourzan

For permission, please contact justateacherbook@gmail.com.
ISBN: 0990991601
ISBN 13: 9780990991601

Printed by: CreateSpace

For Idris and Quillian,
my best teachers

$\mathscr{A}$ B O U T $\mathscr{C}$ H E $\mathscr{A}$ U T H O R

Each of us is a book waiting to be written, and that book,
if written, results in a person explained.

Thomas M. Cirignano

$\mathscr{D}$avid **Tourzan** has taught public school math and science for almost twenty years and has received over $100,000 in grants and awards for innovative programs. In addition to cofounding the Outdoor Discovery Program in southern Oregon, he founded Oregon's first biodiesel company and serves as board president for the local nonprofit Farm to School Program. As cofounder and president of the nonprofit Grandmothers Empowerment Project, Tourzan has distributed over $60,000 to local Native American elders. Tourzan has a master's degree in special education from Portland State University and a bachelor's degree in psychology from Reed College. He is a proud father of two boys, and his wife is a public school Waldorf kindergarten teacher.

$\mathcal{C}$ONTENTS

What the teacher is, is more important than what he teaches.

Karl A. Menninger

$\mathcal{P}$ R E F A C E

The art of teaching is the art of assisting discovery.

Mark Van Doren

Like the stranded Japanese fighter pilot years after the war ended, I thought I was just a teacher for almost two decades. Changing demographics and outdated educational pedagogies, however, were more powerful than my best intentions. I wanted to change the world, but my blossoming youthful idealism threatened to myelinate into the wizened bark of an ancient redwood. I was like a vegan McDonald's, a zafu La-Z-Boy, a homeopathic arthroscopic surgeon—not quite a fish out of water, but steadily swimming upstream.

I taught homeschoolers, unschoolers, one-room schoolers, at-risk, inner-city, suburban, rural, mountain kids, Title I, second-language learners, students with disabilities, and I even tutored rich kids in my life as an educator. Just like that fighter pilot after his respite, by taking a break from teaching and taking time to reflect, I have allowed myself to be more than just a teacher. I have tried to puzzle it together before the details are lost in old journals and notes from my students.

Academics call this metacognition, and philosophers call it existential inquiry. Simpleminded people know that ignorance is bliss, and most of us are too busy just keeping up with life to risk questioning our careers, intentions, and roles in this changing world. Be forewarned; I do not believe everything I think, and I do not know the moral of this story. My hope is that by writing and reflecting on my life as a teacher, I will find my own meaning, and it will be a different lesson for everyone who joins my journey. We all share our mortal desires and fears in such primal ways that even myriad expressions cannot mask the unity in diversity. Although I focus on teaching in southern Oregon, my story is about the bittersweet archetypes that make all life universal.

This is not a book about pedagogy or a peer-reviewed, data-driven analysis of best practices. This heartfelt expression of my decades in the public school classroom is a message in a bottle that may inspire some hope for change. I have included many anecdotes from fellow teachers, masters of their crafts, who have dedicated their whole lives to other people's children. We are all deeply concerned about the state of public education in this country. There are as many ideas on how to solve its problems as there are on any other powerful topic.

There are models that have worked, but how you measure children determines what you consider successful. Success, as defined by standardized state testing, encourages teaching to the test. If science and social studies tests "do not count" toward your funding status, subjects that determine "success" will inevitably supersede them. Thankfully, not all life can be measured by a computer, statistics, or even words. We in the West have been taught to measure ourselves by our individual accomplishments, but some cultures value the family, the elders, or just a state of being above the doings of self. Statistically speaking, one anecdote will outweigh a mountain of data, so I present this qualitative analysis of purely anecdotal evidence in hopes of creating positive change.

I hope prospective teachers will gain a clearer idea of what this career truly entails. I hope that policy makers will learn the subtleties and intricacies of students' stories. Lastly, I want parents and other teachers to find some inspiration, some hope, and maybe some concrete ideas for how to pursue this service work with passion. I do not claim to have all the answers or to be the best teacher ever, but I want to share the students' perspectives, which we rarely hear in the national education debates. I know that students can be our best pedagogical teachers if we just open ourselves to their lessons.

1

A Better Way

If you don't agree, present what you think is a better way.

Steve Scalise

Moving from war-torn Iran to the ivory tower of the Bay Area's yuppie green lawns in third grade, our hot tub was the most heated event I had to survive. Although every family has problems, it took years of teaching the children of the trailer parks to show me that I was definitely a child of privilege. Multicultural atheist immigrants are not America's most popular demographic, so my childhood was a process of transplanting my roots into foreign soil.

After all, I am an immigrant—a hybrid, a transplant, a prodigal son—losing an accent, mocking a language, mocked in prejudices. We moved from Iran during the hostage crisis of 1979 and lost all connection with our extended family, language, and culture. My American friends and I would jokingly call each other racial slurs, never admitting the pain it reflected and projected. We were not particularly proud to be Persian, Korean, or Chinese.

Though we had all the trappings of privilege, a thirst for our own cultures remained dry. We were not even taught our native tongue, since assimilation was the goal. We sang "Ahab the Arab," joked about my dad's accent, and accepted "sand nigger" and "towel head" as normal. Although tolerance is more prevalent today, I still hear certain students using racist slurs that they must have learned at home, and anti-Muslim sentiment abounds.

My British mother openly criticized American culture, and I always felt there had to be a better way. I always felt a little different and that the world must have gone astray sometime in the past, yet we all just followed blindly. In middle school, I loved to study history and discover where we had gone wrong, and most kids have a similar intuition. Adults act as though they know what they are doing, but they cannot admit our societal insanity. I knew I would not be tricked into the mass delusion of group hypnosis; somehow I had to remember this feeling—as Steve Jobs said, "There has to be a better way." Millions of us know this is true right now.

These impulses have been the source of my cognitive dissonance with society, and the zeitgeist of my search for unity in this dualistic world. This was also the clichéd reason for my becoming a teacher—to make the world a better place by empowering children to see behind the curtain. I do not believe in some vast conspiracy with grinning, hand-wringing bald men plotting the enslavement of the entire human population, but I have known powerful men who think, "You only live once, and the earth is for the taking." We are all complicit in this grand illusion, leading our children astray while poisoning the very air they breathe.

The only thing that all teachers have in common may be their desire to make the world a better place. I cannot say that all Wall Street bankers, corporate lawyers, or backroom politicians have good intentions, but every teacher I have ever met started down the primrose path of healthy idealism. I still want to believe that most people are doing their best with what they have received, and that even an embezzling trust fund raider justifies his damage through rationalization. The burned-out teacher with a flask in his drawer, the old union curmudgeon who badmouths coworkers and students alike, the old-timer counting her days to retirement who hates her job; we all became teachers because we believed we could change the world. We all know there must be a better way, though we often have diametrically opposed solutions.

2

⁓

CONCRETE JUNGLE

No chains around my feet, but I'm not free.

Bob Marley

*D*riving to college in Oregon felt like leaving California's concrete jungle and returning to Eden, even though a crack whore's pimp mugged me in Portland on my first visit. But that is a different story. The size of the trees and the biggest highway having only four lanes made up for the backwoods conservatism. It took years for my childlike, candy-store mentality to be tempered by the fires of meth houses and the oversized mufflers of Aryan Nations biker gangs. Portland changed more in the 1990s than I did in the same decade, but we both lost our innocence.

Undergraduate school in southeast P-town taught me about home-brewed beer as dark as coffee, drum circles in the chapel, and naked Slip 'N Slides on the front lawn. I also learned about the foundations and decline of Western civilization from Herodotus and Plato to Pascal and William James. I read about the mysterium tremendum, the sanctum sanctorum, and the dialectic method's search for synthesis.

Humanities classes promoted the patriarchal pomp of perceived perpetual progress. White professors espoused the dogma of tolerance, while endangered Republicans and conservatives often cowered from the reverie of decadence. As was my blissfully ignorant style, I thought the heroin junkies on the student union couches were just stoned slackers.

Before graduating, I learned how deep this ancient system runs; to rebuild it, one has to understand and work within it. I also realized I no longer wanted to be a college professor—that to have the most impact on the world, I would need to teach younger children. I volunteered, tutored, babysat, and took extra classes to find the age group that suited me best. Surprisingly, middle school provided the most challenging and rewarding experience, an age group with continuously evolving minds, and a cynical questioning of authority and their own self-identity.

My first year of student teaching, I broke up a fight one day after school, only to have the principal point out the presence of two gang cars, the true supervisors of authority. Warned not to get involved if it happened again, I took a middle-school elbow to the nose in the next day's after-school street basketball game.

Barely older than many of their siblings, dreadlocks to my waist, and peach fuzz still barely covering my cheeks, I watched eighth graders stuck like chained animals in their elementary-size desk chairs. I smelled bubbling hormones stronger than my hippie body odor, and I weighed less than many of my intended pupils, but I possessed the passion of power. I was going to change the world, one opened mind at a time, even if one kid described my garlic breath as "kickin' like Bruce Lee."

How then to open minds while shut in my own world of privileged illusion? Deluded into believing we all have equal opportunity; that we are all essentially the same inside; that we can all love each other unconditionally—I was in for a rude awakening, not just to the realities of the world, but to the fragility of my idyllic world view.

3

GRADUATE SCHOOL OF LIFE

In school, you're taught a lesson and then given a test. In life, you're given a test that teaches you a lesson.

Tom Bodett

I wore a dress to one of my graduate school lectures on diversity and tolerance just to prove a point, but I did not know you could not stick a fork in a plugged-in toaster—literally and figuratively. I had lots of book knowledge, but little practical experience. Biking and busing downtown every day over the narrow Ross Island Bridge and sitting through direct instruction on the benefits of cooperative learning was formative for me. Although my downtown graduate school provided a direct exposure to urban issues, I was still ill prepared for rural realities. Downtown and northeast Portland taught me much more than the suburbs, but I still had to learn about life within Oregon's farms, ranches, and ultimately, trailer parks. I could understand urban poverty in a visceral sense, but had no idea how much more there was to learn.

When I student taught at a northeast Portland kindergarten, kids would show up in dirty clothes, without snacks or socks, and with issues of abuse and neglect. That was the first school where I had to restrain a little girl who completely lost her temper and got violent with her peers, her teachers, and even inanimate objects within her reach. It was emotionally draining, to say the least, but also a rude awakening to the realities that these kids came from. You could not blame a kid who had fetal alcohol syndrome and came from a broken home with abusive caregivers. I tried to empathize, but I had a hard time even understanding how people like that could have so many children with so many different absentee fathers. There were plenty of fantastic, hardworking families in the school too, but most of the teacher's energy went to the neediest children. That is when I decided to dedicate my career to these underserved children. I did not want to teach in an ivory-tower school like mine.

We gather the smallest lessons as teachers and add them all together to help handle the myriad daily challenges of our profession. I will always remember the professor who taught us the trick of taking a two- to three-minute meditation/prayer/relaxation break right in front of fully engaged kids when they might not notice. Just closing the eyes or softening the gaze and altering the breath can help a teacher stay healthy and present, compared to hours of professional development.

These lessons of the heart have brought my students and me a much deeper level of learning than all the chapters of definitions, standards, and testing. It is this deeper connection that is at the heart of all real teaching, and when we model not just how to "do" things, but how to "be" when doing things, we share the essence of life's gifts. If I am stressed and overwork myself, the kids reflect this; the more relaxed and present I am in my own life, the more centered my classroom becomes. It is a balancing act of the highest importance and requires humble lifelong learning.

I will always remember the dad who told me he had shouted and sworn when trying to fix some plumbing, and his son comforted him with, "Try what teacher David does when he is frustrated. Take some deep breaths and a little break." I have no mastery of any psychic powers and often curse my own plumbing, yet I also know that children can feel a teacher's way of being. I aspire to personal growth and integrity in all my thoughts, words, and deeds, especially in class. I have made many mistakes in the classroom and in life, but I have a poster in my class that says, "The only mistakes are the ones we do not learn from." I readily and regularly apologize for lack of planning, lack of patience, lack of communication, or lackluster performance, and I wear my heart on my sleeve. I teach the kids to express their feelings in a positive way and that they can learn something precious from every interaction, no matter how painful it may feel. I will not lecture to kids about cooperative learning as my poor professor did, because not all lessons in graduate school are as pragmatic as getting schooled by life.

4

SUBSTITUTE SADHU

Electric communication will never be a substitute for the face of someone who with their soul encourages another person to be brave and true.

Charles Dickens

The substitute teacher is the sadhu of the teaching world, wandering from place to place with begging bowl in hand, hoping for auspicious offerings from SubFinder. While many first-year teachers go straight for the contract and many districts prefer hiring directly from the student-teaching pool, I needed a break. When I walked the aisle of convoluted headgear for my master's degree at age twenty-three, I had been in school for eighteen continuous years, since age five in England. I had been turning in assignments and enduring a constant stream of homework for almost two decades. I needed some headspace in so many ways.

Although it set back my prospects of a career position in a comfy district with job security, my first and only year of substitute teaching expanded my narrow horizons. From the inner-city northeast Portland charter school, with graffiti on the walls and laptops for all the students, to the timber country middle school that received parent complaints when I mentioned that I lived with my girlfriend, I wore the costume of the day. Like the jack-of-all-trades, the court jester, the honey-do handyman, and the universal shapeshifter, I tested administrations, classroom styles, building designs, and curricula to find my niche.

We were once asked in graduate school to analogize teaching. Our group decided upon a gardener, since every soil, every climate, and every seed is unique. In the case of a substitute teacher, you are a roving gardener, tending others' plots while they are away and observing the effects of their techniques on the ground they have been given. Some turned city dirt into fertile ground, while others let their heirloom seeds crumble into dust.

Woodshop and welding were the hardest substitute jobs I had in Portland, since I had only ever handled one power tool in my life: a circular saw. I trusted the kids when they showed me the glass grinder and the arc welder, and I ended up with only one student with a cut finger. The welding teacher was not impressed, however, when I let some of the kids make throwing stars from the leftover metal pieces. That was the foolishness of youth. When I used the arc cutter to make a snowboarder silhouette, I was told I was the first substitute teacher to actually try the welding equipment. It is humbling to step into a classroom and know little about the subject matter, but even more so to trust students with compressed flammable toxic gases. In hindsight, the throwing stars were a bad call, but what stands out most was the intense taste and smell in my nose from inhaling burned metal shavings all day. I could not get the smell off my clothes and body, then realized that was because it was actually burned into my nose, so it hardly mattered how much I scrubbed the rest of me.

The way a classroom behaved for the substitute teacher was a clear reflection of the master teacher's skill in classroom discipline and organization. Some classes ran as smooth as silken tofu, with students taking roll, following known routines, and learning from creative projects. There were always classes with troublemakers, but the general demeanor and temperament of the classroom was established through conferred power. One master teacher had conferred so much power that her sub plans for her K-2 classroom were simply "ask the second graders," and the day went fine. As much as I learned from the best and worst of my sub days, I knew I wanted the long-term family relationship of a regular classroom teacher.

5

⌒

The First-Year Teacher

Choose a job you love, and you will never have to work a day in your life.

Confucius

*A*fter my first year subbing, I found a full-time job in the southern Oregon mountains, at a little red schoolhouse with fifty kids in kindergarten through eighth grade. I was a twenty-five-year-old idealistic academic with very little real-world experience, yet the job interview entailed teaching a science lesson. The kids wore sunglasses as I modeled the sun, and the kids rotated and revolved around me to get a kinesthetic view of Earth's tilted axis. One town would not even send me an application, since I did not student teach through Southern Oregon University, but the little red schoolhouse gave me the opportunity of a lifetime.

During my first month, a parent advised me to cut my beard, buy some new clothes, and remember that I was from "the other side of the tracks," since I was a "hippie" and her family were "rednecks." She said we would never see eye to eye, but when I left the job years later, she thanked me for being such a passionate, hardworking teacher, even if she disagreed with much of my curriculum and methods. It was so ironic that she never had anything nice to say in five years of teaching, but decided to compliment me when I quit. They were a classic southern

Oregon mountain family who would call their kid in sick whenever it snowed more than five inches so they could go snowmobiling. Since I had no children at the time, I did not understand this at all.

The mom always wore too-small, muffin-top spandex shorts to school, and they did not prioritize schoolwork because they did not believe that higher education was necessary to be successful. They preferred their son learn how to do real work, like turning wrenches, adjusting carburetors, and logging. I, on the other hand, knew very little about such practical matters, though my head was filled with practical knowledge about science, math, and the arts.

This disdain for intellectual knowledge seemed so foreign to me, yet I learned to appreciate parents with no diplomas who wanted their kids to honor the working-class, blue-collar skills that had built their lives. I had never changed my own oil, built my own house, or burned my own garbage in a metal drum, and I was coming from a very different world of academia. My dad was an electrical engineer with a PhD from Manchester University and UCLA, and my mom was a librarian and part-time teacher—neither one could shoot a deer, tie a fishing knot, or fell a tree.

I asked them not to throw plastic in our campfire at a school outing, and they debated with me about the value of landfills versus backyard burn piles. They took deep pride in taking care of their own garbage, and as mountain people, they did not want to rely on society or statistics to know right from wrong. They preferred that their kids learn independence rather than collaboration, and they certainly did not want the government or some liberal teacher telling them how to live.

In my self-righteous, youthful vigor, I could not appreciate this pragmatic approach to life, but knowing so many unemployed psychology and English majors, I saw how owning a big dump truck and hauling rock from your backyard is a perfectly respectable career. I still wanted the students to have all the options that a well-rounded education could afford, but I did not want to devalue their parents as role models.

One conservative Christian kid told me how his family sprayed their used motor oil over their back forty acres, and how it was like fertilizer for the plants. I asked him if he was worried about carcinogenic chemicals in their watershed and spring-fed well, but he was convinced that plants used it all up. Over a decade later, this family converted the old ranch into a "free-range" local cattle operation, selling half carcasses to rich people who wanted local food.

They actually took on the "green" label for their beef, although their version of "free-range" was often within public forestland. I would go on mountain-bike rides through beautiful meadows only to barely avoid being trampled by a stampede of cattle and would stop to swim in creeks, trying carefully to avoid the floating cow pies all over. I learned so much from their kind and humble daughter, who would try to convert me to Christianity, convince me that abortion was murder, and yet make the most sincere Christmas cards and handmade gifts. I kept a photo she took of me snowboarding at the school sled-hill field trip, the same trip in which her dad pulled donuts in the snowy parking lot, with a Suburban full of thrilled children.

In my third year, her dad called me a scumbag at a school-board meeting. I was trying to teach about evolution in science and condoms in middle-school sex ed. Whenever I mentioned a date more than seven thousand years ago, I would have to add, "As most scientists postulate," or provide an alternative curriculum for the Bible literalists. When I used the word "condom" in eighth-grade health, I defined it as "what married people use when they have intercourse and do not want to get pregnant." This was not as strange to me, though, as the Christians in the rural outskirts of Portland who spoke in tongues and kissed snakes at church.

I had only read about these things in books, but here I was caught between the rednecks and the hippies, flying my freak flag high. I felt caught in the cross fire, and I was not always diplomatic. I ended up bringing the school a new greenhouse, a recycling and compost program, an Internet lab, and tens of thousands of dollars in grants. They left me with the sweetest memory of the best school in the world.

They had a Christmas play where the whole student body became elves and bunnies, and the whole community came out to do lights, sound, costumes, props, and even guest directing. The third through fifth-grade teacher would rewrite her quiver of plays each year to match every child in the school and then play piano all the next morning while kids exchanged handmade gifts. The students knew the second and third verses to all the songs, and Pat could play exquisitely with both hands, leading the whole school in rounds. I asked them to call it the *Winter Play*, and we added some multicultural songs as well. Several parents thanked me for including their traditions for the first time in the school's history. Christmas is great, and there is still a lot of room for Hanuramakwanzamasolstice and Diwali, too.

I was a little sanctimonious, being straight out of graduate school with a vegan chip on my shoulder. I once told the other teachers I thought cows were the biggest blight on our planet, to which they laughed heartily and recommended I keep that opinion to myself in timber and ranch country. I had been to school but had so much more to learn about life.

They were very tolerant of my exuberant, opinionated honesty, and I learned so much from those master teachers, who never lost their cool in front of the kids, ran tight ships, and showed such love and care to all around them. When given a hand-quilted blanket for my first son, I asked if it was for the changing table, completely ignorant of the work that goes into hand stitching such art. I kept that quilt up on my son's door through his teenage years, and I will probably give it to my grandkids someday. I will always aspire to be like Pat and Laurie, who could teach three grade levels each and run a spaghetti dinner with their eyes closed. The whole community was filled with characters from a Steinbeck novel, from loggers and ranchers, to real life miners living in shacks.

Frank was the eighty-seven-year-old ex-timberman living in the back house on the school property. He always joked about me needing to cut my beard, too, but also told me stories about skinning skunks in World War II to make money. He said he could work for two dollars a day cutting timber, but also got two dollars a skunk for their pelts. He figured out a way to bathe them in bleach after trapping them, which would rid them of any smell, and probably burn a few nose hairs too. He grew his gargantuan tomatoes inside old tire stacks and poured Miracle-Gro in them like it was water. He swore like a sailor and told stories like one too.

I distinctly remember when I was teaching sixth- through eighth-grade math, and one of the kids ran up to the window, pointing and screaming, "Frank's got a gun." Sure enough, Frank had caught a raccoon trying to eat his tomatoes and decided to shoot him while he had him trapped. He was incredulous when Pat asked him to wait until the kids were gone, but his heart was in the right place; he did not shoot the coon during school hours.

Frank was the beginning of my learning the benefits of extracurricular involvement for the community. Everyone on the mountain would help him out and check on him, and though most disagreed with his views and found him abrasive, he was a key part of building community. We were all concerned as his health deteriorated, and when he was finally dragged off the mountain after spending thirty hours prostrate where he fell in his kitchen, he died soon after. He taught me that building community was not always easy or pretty, and often required struggle.

So did the year I spent every Saturday building a school greenhouse. The students initiated this project, but many were more concerned with getting their name on the dedication plaque than actually showing up to work. My main helper was a parent named Ted, living with his whole family in his woodshed while building his own house for his wife and three kids. I will always appreciate a guy who takes five years to build his own house in the mountains, but takes a year of Saturdays to design and build a crazy, passive-solar school greenhouse at four thousand feet.

He was the first guy I ever met who said, "God Bless You," at the end of every phone call. No one had ever said that to me before. At first, my nonconformist mind reacted with, "What a bold presumption that I believe in your patriarchal God," and coming from any other person with any other tone, it would have been rejected. Coming from Ted, it was like a precious ointment running over my beard and garments. I was opening my heart to a true Christian, one whose actions spoke louder than his humble offering of kind words.

A middle schooler with an absentee father joined us almost every Saturday. He taught me the value of extracurricular projects for at-risk kids. These Saturdays were much more than a greenhouse project for Tim; they were like a father he never met. For me, they were just some cuckoo freakin' pipe dream of a rookie teacher and some idealistic kids, but whenever I saw Tim years later, he always reminded me that what we built still stands.

He was of mixed ethnicity also, and we shared stories of the pride and prejudice that comes with being different. I still have the card he gave me when he graduated high school, thanking me for changing his attitude toward school, which is the most precious gift a teacher can share. Tim reminded me so much of myself that it took all my willpower to treat him equally to the other students in his class. He had anger issues also, and I would have dreams where he would accost me, being bigger and burlier than my vegan frame. He shared in private what it was like to be of mixed race in a white-bread community, and how kids would call him "a sand nigger" when he went to rodeos in northern California. I could relate so much, and I wanted to take him in my arms like his father never did and tell him that it would be all right. Instead, I had to give him the professional one-arm hug and tell him, "Get used to it, for this is the world you will change."

6

Summer-Break Jobs

I long to accomplish a great and noble task, but it is my chief duty to accomplish humble tasks as though they were great and noble. The world is moved along, not only by the mighty shoves of its heroes, but also by the aggregate of the tiny pushes of each honest worker.

Helen Keller

All the extra hours that teachers put in during the school year are balanced by the fringe benefit of having summers off, but most teachers I know work second and third jobs over the summer to make ends meet. I was at a teacher in-service where teachers described what they did over the summer. The positions ranged from summer-camp coordinator to technology director of the local youth center (yours truly). One teacher took the cake when she said she delivered pizzas over the summer. We all sat there in silent disbelief, not knowing whether to feel admiration or despair, then she broke the punchline and said she had actually taken the summer off. We were all somewhat embarrassed to be in a profession where your master's degree still leaves you cleaning houses or stacking rocks (two of my close friends), and where delivering pizzas is an acceptable night job.

I had a full-time summer job for my first decade of teaching. For several years, I had the privilege of working with the same nonprofit, coordinating their multicultural summer camp. From crawling on the floor like endangered African lions to sweating in a computer lab with thirty third graders bicycling across Africa, I have done it all for twenty-five dollars an hour. I felt guilty asking so much from a nonprofit, but I have a master's degree, eighteen years of continuous schooling, and plumbers still make more per hour.

I loved the nonprofit Kids Unlimited that ran the summer program, and I was amazed at the community support their multicultural camp received. Each week focused on a different continent and included art, theater, dance, music, sports, technology, and field trips. Tom Cole, its founder, cut his teeth at Boys & Girls Clubs. He took this knowledge to the next level, renovating an old bank, then a donated bowling alley, literally raising the roof more than thirty feet to accommodate several indoor basketball courts and performance centers. They offered their after-school programs at all the district schools and included homework support, hands-on help with science, art, sports, and music, and even free food. Some of the kids ate breakfast, lunch, and dinner at the school, and Kids Unlimited provided a safe, supportive place to keep kids off the streets or from being home alone.

Tom's main trick was that the kids thought they were there to play basketball, learn new DJ software, or get free food. Little did they know what else he was teaching them. They were required to maintain a certain GPA to be on the basketball team, had to finish their homework before playing on the computers, and had to show respect to the other kids, volunteers, and staff. We worked with second- and third-generation gang kids, who had to put themselves to bed because their parents worked two jobs with a night shift, and kids who were the first in their family to graduate high school and then college. Tom's program was sheer genius, and he would not be stopped by lack of funding, short-sighted administrators, zoning issues, or even long bureaucratic agenda items.

When I first started my summer job upstairs in the old bank building on Main Street downtown, we had no air conditioning and twenty computers running full speed for four hours at a time. With twenty hot, sweaty kids in there, it felt like a sauna. Actually, that's way too dry, it was more like a steam room. We set up big fans and tried to blow the air into the hot hallway, but as anyone who has been stuck inside a hot building knows, fans can only move air, not cool it. The kids' faces would be red, and the camp counselors who brought their groups would stand in the doorway or next to a fan while I ran around clicking each mouse, unfreezing programs, and reapplying my deodorant. I loved the challenge, and most of these kids had never used a computer, heard of an impala (the animal), or spoken Swahili. They made my summers very busy—over one hundred elementary kids a day—but also very fulfilling.

Some summers, however, we went to music festivals, the Oregon Country Fair, Yosemite, Tahoe, Black Butte, Crater Lake, and weddings. Not exactly relaxing, but still fulfilling to the soul and family. I played a few gigs and had the contrasting experience of going from working six out of seven days to traveling six out of seven days. We were home for one day, just long enough for laundry, plant watering, and chicken adoption, then gone again for six or more. It was fun because life is short and you have to make the most of each breath. Very few people die wishing they had worked more hours.

At the Oregon Country Fair, we saw giant puppets, naked mud parades, break-beat Buddhas, and a show where more than half the audience was curled in a fetal position under blankets. I wandered at a snail's pace around a magical mobius and found myself under the stars of eternity, wondering how to create my own reality with the experiences that I need. I often wondered what my students would think if they knew my secret identity or saw me in a loincloth in the Dragon Parade. I liked being a secret subversive, subtly swerving society toward sustainability.

Even a couple of weeks before school started, I still had no lesson plans, but I had my sanity, my inspiration, and my will to inspire wisdom among the youth. I had the moisture to sweeten the seed of fruitless pursuits. Students reflect teachings as the turbulent waters absorb the visage of nature's patterns. I tried to reflect the teachings to channel the stream's current, and taking a summer off from teaching helped me stay in the flow.

7

BACK TO SCHOOL

He who opens a school door, closes a prison.

Victor Hugo

Everyone is nervous on the first day back to school, including the teachers. They say not to smile until Christmas, but I always preferred the humanitarian approach to the first day, with get-to-know-you games and letting kids come up with some classroom rules themselves. The new kids look like deer in the headlights, afraid to speak or move for fear of the hunting sights of judgmental peers. They show up with their best duds on, their new shoes, their latest digital devices, and a summer's worth of academic regression.

If we are lucky, the teachers come back with rested minds, new inspirations, and the patience to start the year on a new foot. In wealthier school districts, you might hear about kids' trips overseas and fun summer camps, but many kids talk about the boredom of nothing to do, watching TV, and hanging out at the mall. Quite a few kids always say they could not wait to come back to school because their lives are so boring there is nothing to do when school is out. As much as I feel proud to be the center of their overscreened lives, I simultaneously feel sorry for kids who lack the support and inspiration to find joy in their time off.

Then, of course, there are the kids who eat three meals a day at school and use the aftercare program until 6:00 p.m., who have had to fend for themselves all summer. Families who cannot afford the YMCA or the Boys & Girls Club often leave their children in the care of a neighbor, older cousin, or grandparent, while all kids lose retention of information over the summer. Involved parents make sure their kids keep up with reading and maybe even a little math over the summer, but many are too busy, too tired, or ill informed about the benefits to follow through. There is so much that parents can do to help their children retain skills over the summer, and the resulting benefits far outweigh the new shoes or brand-name sweatshirts pushed in back-to-school advertising.

My neighbors in Portland had three kids who had never been camping in their lives. They had never been on a hike, not even to Mount Tabor or Forest Park, a one-dollar bus ride away. They loved their kids and worked hard to provide for them, but they did not provide many extracurricular activities. They spent more time watching TV than outside with the kids, and they spent more money on beer than family trips. But those kids always looked sharp on the first day of school, and that meant a lot to them.

As important as deep breaths, lesson plans and procedures are on that first day back, I find the most important factor is the rest and readiness of the teacher. For years, I would work the entire weekend before the first day of school, spending hours in my classroom getting everything perfect, but being exhausted. I still overprepare to handle my worries about the first day, but I now take as much time as possible for my family and myself on the weekend before returning to the all-consuming task of teaching.

8

~

Why Am I Here?

An idealist is a person who helps other people to be prosperous.

Henry Ford

*I*t was hard to maintain my idealism in the face of reality, but that is the true task of life, of every parent who ever dreamed of a better life for his or her child. It requires support in every realm, from the familial to the spiritual. Words and stories can support us in our struggle to maintain a spiritual reality in this world of material illusion. By writing, I remind myself why I am here, and I hope to spark some flame of recognition within our collective self. We know our purpose is to serve others with the gifts we are given, but wonder how?

We eat canned food, live fast lives, drink soft drinks, use instant messaging, and get a canned attitude. Despite mass marketing, the alignment of my assignment is defined by what the signs meant. The good in everyone's story is symbolic of life's struggle to grow. Some stories are painful, some hopeful, but they are all true and from the heart.

Rob was the first middle-school student who ever wrote me an invitation letter when he graduated from high school. The kid was big, easily the biggest kid in his whole middle-school class of twelve students. That was the difference when you went to the little red schoolhouse; as much as the postcard cliché was beautiful, it was flawed like us all. He was never popular, but he had an intelligence and integrity that shone through his awkwardness. I went to the graduation and saw his drywaller dad and waitress mom in complete bliss as their eldest son walked proudly across the stage. It is hard to overstate the importance of such small victories in the face of daunting odds. Whether high school or college, I have seen so many kids become the first in their family to graduate, and each time is like the first. Rob had two supportive, hardworking parents, and that helped a lot.

Rob's younger brother Mike once broke his arm trying to do a backflip off the swing after I had done it the day before. I had to drive him down the thirty-minute trip to the hospital, while he tried not to go into shock or vomit in the car. It was quite a bonding experience because we were both scared speechless by the bulge in his arm. Mike was a smart kid also, but he always struggled to keep up with Rob's hard work. I saw him a decade later, working at a trade show, but he had a very unfortunate fetish for firearms that cut his life short. He is my only student who passed in this way, and I will always feel sad for him and his family. Even within families, so much is beyond our control. Even within our own lives, we cannot control all circumstances, just our reactions.

Mike is not the only student of mine who has died, though the only one I know who took his own life. Knowing children with terminal illnesses is an inevitable part of working with thousands of kids over one's career. It is the one part of teaching that no words can help. Sometimes it takes years like cancer, then other times it changes in one day like a car accident. No matter the circumstances, the pain and confusion makes everything else seem futile. I can only try to put on a brave face for the kids, go home and hold someone I love. I will never get used to this aspect of teaching and my deepest condolences go out to anyone who has experienced this worst of all losses. These losses can break up a family., but there are no broken families, just family patterns that can be broken with enough love, self-reflection, and hard work.

Billy never really knew his dad, although he had heard a lot about him. As a baby in Mexico, he had to see his father beat his mother every day, but he does not remember him beyond that. When Mom moved them to the United States, Billy became the man of the house. He started hanging out with older kids and liked to drink on the weekends. I took him to the skate park with my kids, and he biked around while we skated. He was a smart, polite young man when he needed to be. His older sister hung around a rough crowd and may have had gang associations, but their mother was trying to hold true to their traditions and culture. You could see in Billy's eyes that he had seen a lot of life in his short time on this planet. He did not need to say much to mean a lot. He ended up graduating, getting a solid job as a mechanic, and breaking the family pattern of drunken, abusive, negligent fathers. He mostly had his mother to thank for that, but I also know that school for him was an escape, a rare oasis in his desert of poverty.

There are so many kids for whom school is their one predictable, stable, and constructive influence. It is so easy to get lost in the curriculum and the standards, we sometimes forget why we became a teacher in the first place. We help kids to prosper, whether as mechanics or engineers, and we help families to improve their lives. At times in my life I have been so focused on a particular career goal that I have missed ripe opportunities right in front of me, but I know that underserved kids with high needs are in every school, on every continent of this teeming world.

9

UNSCHOOLING HANDOFFS

When you are safe at home, you wish you were having an adventure, and when you are having an adventure, you wish you were safe at home.

Thornton Wilder

After the birth of our first son, my wife and I decided to both work part-time and share the joys of parenthood together. Because of the long commute and even longer work hours, I left the little red schoolhouse and found part-time work at a "homeschool support" program offered through the local public school. I also tutored and taught at the local science museum and through the university extension programs. I had four part-time jobs, sometimes all in one day, and that did not count handing off the baby to Leann. This was not exactly how I had envisioned my job-sharing, but at least I could spend a lot more time with my newborn than most fathers.

Our overlapping schedules left one day each week where she ended her class at 12:30 and mine began at 12:30, and I literally would hand her the baby and walk into the next full classroom to teach. It looked good on paper, but my ideal balanced life with an independent working spouse was more like a frantic juggling circus. Each day, we'd look at each other and wonder who was making dinner that night, whose turn it was to put the baby to bed, and who we were tomorrow. Luckily, our first child was a relative angel, and I relish those two years I spent with him as primary caregiver along with Leann. It was a rare privilege, and though we barely made ends meet and frantically juggled jobs and breast pumps, I am glad we gave it a try. There is no ideal model for shared parenting, and we had to break the mold.

The homeschooling support program was inventive because I got to write and propose my own classes, from a role-playing social studies class based on kids reading *Guns, Germs, and Steel* to a physics class based on da Vinci's inventions. I really appreciated the lack of focus on standardized testing, but I was unprepared for the unschooling movement, one that actually believes that all teaching should be the choice of the child. If a child does not want to learn to read, so went the thinking, he or she should not be forced; the same goes for times tables, science, art, or anything else that does not interest the child. Sometimes I would have an unschooler in my class, and I could not require homework since the parents would not enforce something the kid did not want to do. I would have that kid in the same class with a right-wing Christian conservative who would call me "Sir." There were involved students from the unschooler and Christian groups, but I quickly realized that some students would always want more homework and some always less. I tried to meet all their needs, even if I disagreed with them. I tried to be flexible, but also assertive about my requirements.

I really appreciated the alternative angle that this program put forward about public support of homeschooling. They moved from a closet in the middle school to their own campus, with a multimillion-dollar barn/theater remodel, riparian area rehabilitation, and a new playground, parking lot, and community garden. Each child could take only a limited number of classes per day, as it was intended for homeschool support. Though teachers were paid an hourly wage with no benefits, the program provided a flexible, creative, and social support for homeschoolers. It provided Leann and me with flexible teaching schedules that could meet our desire to coparent, even if we could not afford medical insurance.

One of the main challenges for parents working part-time and sharing parenting responsibilities is the lack of health insurance. It is very expensive to get health insurance for a part-time employee, even in teaching, and being uninsured feels very risky in this country. My mom always reminds me that in England people do not live in fear of medical bankruptcy. My dad reminds me that most of the world's citizens have never had insurance, but with kids and a home to protect, it feels necessary. Maybe I am getting schooled by fearmongering salespeople and could use a little unschooling myself.

I was tired of eating lunch in my car on the way to the next job. Most days, I would have only fifteen minutes to make it to the next job, and I would try to inhale my sandwich while driving with the other hand. There were many cucumbers between the seats and spilled tea. Some days, I would watch my son for three hours, tutor two kids, run over to teach an after-school science program, eat a quick dinner, and then teach a night school SAT class.

I kept telling my wife that I was able to move very quickly on the outside and only appeared frantically crazed, but that inside I was maintaining a Zen-like calmness. I was trying to master the act of moving quickly but thinking slowly, which I still think is possible, but driving in traffic when running late requires some serious detachment that I do not have. I was so concerned about punctuality and professionalism that I would swerve in and out of traffic while eating my lunch in an adrenaline-fueled frenzy. I offered a sliding scale for tutoring, but parents always chose the lowest rung, even if they had a new Mercedes in the driveway. Leann wanted to focus on creating an at-home preschool, and we needed the income and insurance, so I decided it was time to go back to work full-time.

10

MASS CONFUCIAN

I believe in stopping work and eating lunch.

L'Wren Scott

Full time teaching for me is like swimming through an ocean, trying to stay afloat until the next island. I have never been able to pull off project-based teaching in less than 50 hours a week, but often would approach 60 hours on a bad week. I often felt adrift along the shores of time. How many years have I ferried across the river? How many lifetimes have I drowned in the storm? I am but a mortal, a sentient being, whorled in samsara, world in inertia. Sometimes, I felt like a mad Confucian, secretly teaching through mass confusion.

We have no model for our age, no *Leave It to Beaver* paradigm of the ideal family. I was taught that a woman should have a career and be independent so she does not rely on the man for all her security in life. My wife was taught a Catholic version of "Stand by Your Man," which kept her parents together until the end. We tried the nontraditional job-sharing method, and it was rewarding but exhausting. We did not realize that we were about to jump into a decade of old-fashioned "man gone all day" method of madness, which began when I got a job at a school for at-risk middle and high schoolers.

While this particular charter school started as a Talented and Gifted and homeschool support program, it quickly became a place for kids who did not fit into the mainstream schools for a variety of reasons. The administrative structure made all teachers equal codirectors, and we shared the administrative and office duties equally. I really liked their democratic methods, although consensus decision-making can be very challenging. I prefer consensus minus one so that one individual cannot hold up a decision. Actually, I prefer very few meetings at all, since my bottom starts to hurt after one hour. I have to stand up and wiggle to pay attention, much like the students at this school.

I probably have undiagnosed ADHD (attention-deficit hyperactivity disorder), because I listen better while doodling, my typewriter leg taps a constant rhythm when sitting, and I prefer calm music in the background when I write, read, or do lesson plans. I think that having tons of energy is a benefit, but I also know that I have had to create many ways to accommodate my hyperactivity. I use daily meditation and regular exercise to focus my boundless energy, but my body does not like to sit still for more than one hour. This helps me relate to the countless restless boys, who need movement to learn.

We had many meetings where people stormed out in tears or tossed things across the table, and that was quite a rude awakening for a guy who thought *Robert's Rules of Order* were like law. I learned so much from these veteran teachers, and even though I disagreed with some of their theories, I will always admire their dedication and perseverance in the face of such daunting stories. I wrote more unbelievable anecdotes in those few years of teaching trailer kids than in all my other years of inner-city, suburban, and rural teaching combined.

Their best tradition was for the whole faculty to eat out every half-day Friday for lunch before we returned to our afternoon faculty meeting. Now, Phoenix, Oregon, is not a culinary capital, so we chose Sue's Diner, the Pilot truck stop, and even Chang's Chinese American Restaurant. For a recovering militant vegan, I had to really open my mind to the experience and get used to a lot of indigestion. I have to admit that it was my first truck-stop dining experience, and when a fellow teacher, Kathie, bought a "spinner" hubcap necklace, we dared her to wear it to school on Monday. We laughed, shared stories, and ate overfried food because the company was more nourishing than the food.

My old judgmental ways were giving way to the down-to-earth realities of my students, and I even took a struggling kid to Jack in the

Box and ate a fish burger to prove I was not a total organic hippie freak. The Gospel of Thomas says that it is not what enters the mouth that pollutes our souls, but what comes out of the mouth. So I tried to embody that spirit, with a wing and a prayer, as I swallowed my pride and my principles to meet people where they were. I needed to understand my students, and while I did not make it a habit, eating with them, sharing my organic tofu sandwiches and their soggy French fries, was often more significant to them than my grandiose speeches.

11

Coping Machinations

More men are killed by overwork than the importance of the world justifies.

Rudyard Kipling

Having a personal connection with students is a double-edged sword. It can change kids lives, but can also be a heavy burden. Sometimes I would come home and could not stop thinking about a kid at school. During those years, thoughts of troubled students even haunted my dreams. I started coping by drinking a couple of glasses of wine to help smooth the transition, and this rapidly digressed to a full bottle—organic, of course. A full bottle of wine in a stressed-out belly is a bitter fruit, so I made the diversion into tequila—Patr n Añejo, of course. While the alcohol drastically reduced my dwelling on student issues, it also severely diminished my desire to exercise, read books, and, especially, correct math assignments with sloppy accuracy. I would work until I was physically unable to continue, stopping only from total exhaustion, double vision, or falling asleep with a stack of corrections in my lap.

Partial inebriation often gave me the ability to work five twelve-hour days and still play joyfully with my child during my one-hour break after dinner. I would too often find myself playing Legos and thinking about some kid at school, until a certain stupor helped me forget all I needed to get done. Imbibing also allowed me to do monthly business accounting at 9:00 p.m., when my physical body was feeling the weight of Earth's attraction. Of course, the true sadhu reaches these states without external aids, and yet I doubt they had sixty-hour-a-week jobs and families. At this point in life, I still had four jobs: full-time teaching, part-time biodiesel management, property management, and non-profit presidency, not to mention being a father and husband. In winter, I would leave the house in the dark of the morning before the kids were awake and come home when it was dark again, and they were just sitting down for dinner. I know there are people who work way harder than that and seem to cope just fine. I also know a lot of people lean on alcohol when exhausted from work, and that many teachers rely too strongly on this coping mechanism.

How would a mathematician write a formula for a workaholic justifying his or her vices with long hours? It's called a null set, so I stopped drinking several years ago, ran a few marathons, and tried not to work past 10:00 p.m. anymore. Teaching can be an all-consuming profession, where sudden intuitive ideas come at a gift shop on vacation, lying in bed at night, or while playing with my own children. There is always something to do, and the feeling of never catching up must be tempered with knowing when enough is enough. I prided myself on always returning students' work the next day, but sometimes I had to give myself a break, so I could still be centered and patient. It is hard to find that balance before burnout and is probably why the majority of teachers quit within five years.

I know some teachers who commit to never showing up more than one hour before and never working more than one hour past contractual hours, but that has never worked for me. I know some teachers who refuse to do any work on weekends, but my wife gave me four hours every Sunday to "catch up." I loved staying up late making up new projects, researching new field studies, or just reading kids' papers. However, 10:00 p.m. has to be my limit. On good days, I do not work from 5:00 p.m. to 8:00 p.m., instead helping with dinner and bedtime, then picking up the pad and pen from 8:00 p.m. to 10:00 p.m. Balancing life and work is not well modeled in our society, and I have erred on the side of teaching my kids a strong work ethic. As I have learned so well with my own children, however, they do not always learn the same lesson you are teaching.

Maybe I have also taught them how to neglect their own personal needs, how to be distracted and distant from their own children, and how to put more time and energy into their jobs than their families. I tried to model punctuality with my family, and now my oldest son complains that we are late if we are not five minutes early, so I am learning to question my assumptions about the lessons I am really teaching. I do not want my kids to repeat my mistakes, so I have to keep learning from them instead of assuming I am always right because it has worked for me. Children are the ultimate gift of self-reflection, as improving our parenting is such a humbling process when approached with love. My kids have taught me more about myself than all the shelves of philosophy, psychology, biology, or spirituality I have ever read. They are not the center of my life, but they definitely help bring me opportunities to balance and center myself on a daily basis.

After four miscarriages, my wife gave birth to our second son. He was born eight weeks premature, and we had to spend thirty-five days in the NICU (Neonatal Intensive Care Unit). Our little man had tubes up his nose and in his arms, and he had beeping machines and top-forty radio playing way too loud. He was born on a Friday, and because of the lack of substitutes and my workaholic tendencies, I went back to work full-time on Monday. I thought I was being strong, providing for my family, and fulfilling my professional duties, but in retrospect, it was totally obsessive and unfair to my wife. My dad came up to help with my older son, but we basically lived in a halfway house just outside the hospital and spent every waking moment holding, breathing, and having skin-to-skin contact with our struggling infant.

I was actually losing my mind, my battle with alcohol, and my grip on reality, but somehow I managed to show up, do my job, and still hold my baby until midnight every night. My goddess warrior wife had to set an alarm to wake up every three hours and pump her breast milk so that our son could be fed from a nasal tube, since he was "too little" to properly latch on and nurse. I would try to wake up and support her, but having to get to work the next day, I was hardly present at 3:00 a.m. I still regret my prioritizing work, but we needed the paycheck, and I thought I was doing the right thing at the time.

I have since learned how painful this time was for her, feeling very alone, disconnected by my daily absence, but also lucky to have the resources to provide for not only our child but for many others who lacked breast milk. Many were forced to drink the factory-farmed formula. We still see a couple of the kids who have Leann's blessed breast milk in their bones. While she was dealing with life and death issues at the hospital, I was trying to make it through the end of the school year without taking too many sub days. I still see those teachers and just shake my head in wonder that we made it through that exhausting episode. It was like living in 2 worlds, both foreign and dreamlike in their intensity.

12

RANDOM OPPORTUNITIES

There are people in the world so hungry that God cannot appear to them except in the form of bread.

Mohandas Gandhi

Assigned to write about his dreams, Mike wrote that he wanted to kick my ass because I was such a pussy. I asked for advice from a veteran teacher who said, "Well, if it's not a death threat, then I wouldn't really worry about it." I was shocked at the time but realized later it is impossible to have zero-tolerance policies when every kid is so unique. Later that year, Mike wanted to Hacky Sack with me, asked how he was doing in my class, and even turned in one extra-credit article. He might have ended up dropping out of our school, but I hoped he learned something in the process. He had that classic fetal-alcohol-syndrome look—very pale, big ears, bad teeth, and very small for his age. After he misbehaved in class for the millionth time, I called his mom in for a conference, at which she asked him, "Why are you so f—king retarded?" She threatened to "beat his ass" when they got home, and she did not help at all. He was not better behaved the next day, but like a beaten dog, he came back in with a tail-between-the-legs vengeance and an understandable resentment.

That was the last time I called his mom about his misbehavior. I realized I was probably better off trying to handle it myself. I could hardly blame this kid, since he had no positive role models, but I told him that at a certain point he could not blame his mom, his lack of a dad, or his learning disabilities for his failures. Even a kid from this background had to take his life into his own hands eventually, and I insisted that he could do better than his own parents had.

Another student, Bob, sat in the office, saying he hated me and hated math class, and he would not do anything that I asked him to do. The codirector of the charter school explained that students had to take directions from any faculty member at any time or else find another school. We had many other battles of will over the next few weeks, but I also took him to lunch, gave him rides home, and shared hip-hop tracks with him. In short, I invested in building a caring relationship, along with stern boundaries. Months later, he made me a Betty Crocker cake for my birthday. It was a microwave recipe his grandmother had passed down to him, complete with buttery blue frosting. My former vegan attitude swallowed its pride and gave thanks for the random opportunity. You never really know what is going to impact a kid's view of school and teachers, but I figured I would take every random opportunity as a blessing, even his grandmother's microwave magic.

What all these kids had in common was the poverty of their trailer-park backgrounds, their absentee or abusive fathers, and their total disinterest in school. I cannot say that one caused the others, and I know quite a few kids from the trailer parks that lead perfectly healthy lives. Too often, however, I saw many of these kids coming in reeking so badly of cigarettes that I had to open a window, even in winter. The kid who "baked" me his grandma's microwave cake helped me install a subwoofer at his "house," and the smell of trash, cigarettes, and stale beer was palpable from the scattered piles. He was such a smart kid in so many ways, but he had such poor hygiene, diet, study skills, and anger management—all things that parents need to teach early in life.

Every child grows up in a culture, and that culture helps foster values for the rest of their lives. The Oregon trailer culture is the poorest one I have ever seen, even compared to the slums of India, the ghettos of Portland, and the barrios of Mexico. It is not simply economic poverty that degrades a child's potential. It is cultural, emotional, and intellectual poverty. A rich child from an abusive home will not have the emotional resilience of a poor child with caring parents. At least the economically poor Hispanic community has its Catholic church, its customs, celebrations, traditional music, work ethic, and family values. The poorest parts of north Portland still have an Ethiopian restaurant, a corner store, a Baptist church, and a strong culture of music, dance, and sports. You may have a crack house on the block, but you also know which neighbor knows about her ancestry, her community, and her history. There are progressive thinkers who seek to vitalize these cultures with positive activism.

I have not seen that same culture in the trailer parks of Oregon. Of course, there are stable families, smart kids, and positive aspects of every community, but I have seen some very scary habits learned in trailer parks. Perhaps it is because I just do not relate to beer-drinking, TV-watching, four-wheeling, fast-food eating, gun-shooting, wife-beater-wearing people of any culture. Do not get me wrong; I can handle all those things in moderation—except wife beaters—and I have tried them all in my life, but they are by no means the foundation of a healthy culture. Even those in poverty can create a rich culture. I still know that such mothers love their children. Many of us just never learned the healthiest ways to express that love. I am still learning every day.

The Jesuits say, "Give us a child until he is seven, and we will show you the man." Although I am confident change is possible at any age, brain research confirms that many crucial neural pathways are established at an early age and that the culling of unused synapses and myelination of habitual pathways make patterns for life. I always tell the students that choices become habits, habits become personality, and personality becomes character. Every time we see someone lose his or her temper or allow those pathways to fire in our brains, we strengthen their likelihood to repeat. Every time we are helped to focus on a game, book, or task for extended periods or calm ourselves when upset, we strengthen our hemispheric lateralization, or brain balance.

I know that most parents do their best to love and care for their children, and I believe that given the right tools, most would never choose to harm them. Even the best parents make mistakes, and we are all going to mess our kids up somehow, but the common denominator for success is unconditional love, time and attention, and self-reflection. It is hard to find enough time for a single parent who is struggling just to get by, but luckily, loving parenting does not require much money at all. All the research shows that reading with children nightly at an early age, avoiding fear-based discipline, and paying attention to their schoolwork and grades totally offsets any economic disadvantages in terms of school performance. Almost anyone can do it if we just teach them how, support them in their learning, and celebrate their successes. Of course, this is much more challenging for people with 2 jobs and swing shift, or for a single mom.

1 3

⌒

My Dad's in Jail

I don't miss my dad, because I never really knew him.

Anonymous Student

Asking about a student's parents was like Russian roulette. Sam had not seen his dad since he was three years old, when his mother moved them out of state to escape the father's abusive behavior. Sam's dad said he did not want a kid, and he never wanted to see them again, but Sam might still want to see him someday just to tell him how much of an asshole he is. I really did not know what to say to him about forgiveness or love, so I just listened and tried to be a consistent factor in his life. No dad is perfect, but having no dad is usually worse.

Linda's dad was in jail for shooting someone in a bar fight when she was just five years old. He was down for life, and she would visit him every few years just to stay in touch. "My dad's in jail, but I do not miss him, 'cuz I never really knew him," she explained on the way back from PE. She wanted to hang out in my classroom at lunch, but I remembered my teacher training and never had a female student alone in a room with the door closed. I did let her and another couple of students come in and work on their beats for audio technology class, but they usually just wanted to talk. She was another brilliant girl, being raised by a struggling single mother, who was lucky to have found a program that allowed her to catch up on her credits or get a GED.

The mainstream school system and all teachers struggle to meet the needs of kids working thirty hours a week at Taco Bell, helping out with rent, and coming home to an empty house every night. Our program's night school was always full, though attendance was sporadic. The GED program was dropped because it did not help the district meet the state standards, which made it a "failing" district. Despite the hundreds of kids who found pride and success through a GED, the national "Race to the Top" to "Leave No Child Behind" meant they must all fit the same box.

At the IEP meeting (special education) for Jake, I remarked that his less than 50 percent attendance record was hurting his academic progress. "Were you the one with strep throat this semester?" his mother asked him, confusing sons. I said that he had been vomiting at school, out my back door, after coughing and gagging. His cigarette habit and probable pot smoking, as well as an extra one hundred pounds at age fifteen, did not help. The district staff explained that they were adjusting his medication, and that his mother would help him to change his soda and Doritos breakfast.

The poor kid was happy-go-lucky, but he had no idea how far behind and close to dropping out he was. Jake had been getting language arts credit for writing to his dad in jail, but had very little to say, since writing was such an embarrassing struggle. I told him to record a message, and we would make his dad a CD, but he still wanted to act as if he did not really care. Maybe he did not care, since he had very little faith that any man would follow through on his word or stick around in his life. I knew he was hurting inside and kept looking for ways to break through.

The girls and guys handled the lack of male role model very differently, with the girls clinging desperately to "ballers" and troublemakers and the guys trying to act older than their age and rebelling against any female authorities in their lives. It takes a strong soul to break the family pattern of alcohol, substance, and physical/verbal abuse that has torn so many apart. It also takes a strong community to support them, with highly valued teachers at its heart. Teachers often see straight into the heart of a family's issues.

14

~

METHADEMIC

Addiction isn't about substance—you aren't addicted to the substance, you are addicted to the alteration of mood that the substance brings.

Susan Cheever

The constant jaw twitching, hair flicking, and fast talking were a dead giveaway during the parent-teacher conference. Sasha was obviously embarrassed by her mother when she knocked the lampshade off the teacher's desk with an exceptionally grandiose hair flick. I thought her mom was just nervous, but a veteran teacher debriefed me after the performance. Sasha seemed very centered and would look you in the eye and tell you how she would do extra credit to make up for her absences. Her cards were stacked against her and were leaning toward GED, if not foster care or the streets. Mom wanted to take her out of school for a week because they got free NASCAR tickets. I tried not to judge, but felt really sad and exhausted at the end of the fourteen-hour conference day—from eight in the morning to ten at night—to accommodate working parents. Despite offering such broad hours, some parents still refused to return any forms, attend any meetings, or even call or e-mail to check in. It broke my heart, but I tried to remember that even those parents were doing their best, and better than nothing.

Mike liked to bring his guitar to school, and I had shown him some Bob Marley riffs. I thought he was just a stoner, but he tested positive for meth and would go to residential treatment for probation violation. I was shocked and saddened, but the rest of the veteran faculty assured me that the best thing that could happen to him was getting out of his meth-filled house. Considering the overcrowded state of Oregon facilities, I had never thought that incarceration could be better than home, which just shows how bad his home was. He did not have any of the obvious signs of meth addiction, but as a youngster just starting, the ill effects are harder to see.

Oregon is at the heart of the methademic, and this heartless addiction leaves kids as the unfortunate victims. They never asked to be introduced to this form of pharmaceutical slavery, never asked to be born into a meth trailer. Yet the fruit falls close to the tree, and the best thing for many of these kids is to be removed from their homes. Of course, that does not address the root causes, but capitalism often runs on the trimming of its branches. We spend far more on incarceration than treatment, far more on enforcement than on rehabilitation. Ironically, our "three strikes" laws in Oregon and federal drug laws have left our jails so crowded that common criminals are released because of overcrowding. Recidivism is so high because there are so few support systems for struggling families, and the nanny state and Walmart mentality discourage personal responsibility.

Southern Oregon has billboards showing before-and-after photos of methamphetamine addicts. We have Spanish and English public service announcements stating, "Do not try meth, not even once." I know stories from Child Protective Services about rescuing children from methamphetamine labs where toxic chemicals, flammable off-gassing, and abusive drug addicts are common. I know the pharmaceutical industry fights the law, but ever since the banning of over-the-counter sales of certain cough medicines, much of the meth has been manufactured in supersized Mexican meth factories and shipped up by the truckload. This helped reduce Oregon's production rate, but did not seem to decrease demand. We had crackheads when I was a kid, but it seems that even inner-city drug addicts now prefer methamphetamine, because it is cheaper and the high lasts longer. I know people who started as cute, middle class, and healthy and ended up giving blowjobs in men's restrooms, proudly telling me, "At least I never let them cum in my mouth." These are choices we cannot even imagine making as highly educated professionals, but compassion is still necessary. These people have children, and to teach them, I have to understand them, without judgment. Even when a kid tests positive for meth., I will leave the judgment to the judge.

15

⌒

URINALYSIS

Those who would give up essential liberty, to purchase a
little temporary safety, deserve neither liberty nor safety.

Benjamin Franklin

*A*s codirector of a charter school, you have to do many tasks
you never imagined. Rather than hire outside contractors,
we often split the work among ourselves to save money. Charter schools
are responsible for their own budgets and have to beg, borrow, and
build it while they fly it. This particular charter school helped me learn
accounting, billing, filing, and spreadsheets. I also learned the signs of
abuse, the effects of neglect, and how to perform a urinalysis.

I once stood in a bathroom stall with a scrawny teen named Jim,
while he tried to pee in a cup. He could not pee for two hours as we
all fed him water and Pepsi until his bladder burst. I stood outside the
door to be polite and listen for the obvious signs of dilution; a running
faucet or the requisite dip in the toilet water, but every time he came
up short. Imagine peeing under that much pressure. The last two tries,
I told him stories about my experience with cup filling, and it seemed
to loosen him up. He almost peed when I told him about the Medford
School District policy of urine-testing every applicant before he or she
gets the job, like a guilty criminal before proven innocent. He finally
filled the cup while I told him about my research into how students try

to trick the tests by drinking gallons of water, buying strange concoctions, and even strapping warmed Internet urine to their bellies. The latest gimmick actually involves a fake strap-on penis, so no tubes or caps are seen. Luckily, no one asked me to make sure his penis was real, but it was still a humbling experience for us both.

The best part is that Jim came out clean for meth and pot, the two tests on one dipstick. I appreciated the irony of testing for pot and meth, almost like two ends of the drug spectrum, from the least deadly to the most. It was like waiting for a pregnancy test, watching for one stripe or two to show up in the soak. Jim had just been taken off his meds for ADHD and other special needs, which kept him a four-foot-tall sophomore. His mother requested the drug test after his grades slipped from bad to worse, and he started skipping school. She traveled the world as a hypnotherapist and the kid wore T-shirts saying, "My Mom went to Dubai, and all I got was this lousy T-shirt." He was adopted but did not know it. His adoptive father was deceased, the mother wealthy but distant. I never saw her at a parent-teacher conference and only spoke with her on the phone. He was not your typical southern Oregon born-again type, but more of a Bob Marley–listening class clown with a conscience. He made jokes about "the Man" and his own "vertical challenges," and even when he drove me crazy, I still loved him.

He took this humiliating act of modern septic science with bravado, but I have to laugh at the irony of a piss-tested teacher piss-testing his pissed-off student. If we both came out clean, what did it say about the system's guilt? This system profits from insurance and pharmaceutical corporations that require both citizen oversight and regulation to maintain fairness for working families, elders, and the disabled.

16

～

OREGON HEALTH PLAN

I say everyone should have health care. I'm not selling insurance.

Dennis Kucinich

"I put my granddaughter on birth control to help her acne," the sweet grandma told me in the parking lot of the high school after an IEP (special education) assessment meeting. Turned out that Alyssa was just borderline learning disabled in writing, but she was not disabled enough to receive special services from the district. Her grandma explained that it had been like that her whole life, ever since Alyssa's alcoholic mother got pregnant at sixteen. Alyssa was taken from her mother by the state, and her grandmother, Evelyn, stepped in to take custody.

Evelyn was a sweet, gray-haired elderly woman with a tendency to ramble. She had a lot to talk about with her hands as full as they were. I often had to escape with an excuse or else still be stuck talking an hour later. I had no idea where the father and grandfather were and did not ask.

Evelyn made a little too much money to be on the Oregon Health Plan (OHP) herself, but her two wards of the state (grandchildren) were both enrolled. Unfortunately, OHP did not cover most preventative care and funded only basic needs. Since they would not fund any sort of acne medication for Alyssa, who had been teased since sixth grade about her excessive pimples, Evelyn put her on birth control pills, which were covered. The other teachers reminded me that I should be thankful that at least OHP was progressive enough to fund birth control, and that she was one less girl getting pregnant at sixteen.

Alyssa was a sweet, quiet, artistic girl who made the most amazing avant-garde ambient beats in our music production class. She would make a fifteen-minute sonic journey that really showed how "out there" her imagination was, but would barely whisper an answer in class. Her art, writing, and music set her free, yet these are the least emphasized aspects of modern state testing. Do not get me started on that. I know we need to compete with China, but I will let someone else win the rat race to the bottom if it means we do not have time for art, music, and hands-on learning. Those were the only aspects of school that allowed Alyssa to put up with the rest. What is life without art, and why is the GDP the measure of a culture's success? The way we measure ourselves determines our priorities and values. I know that some of the most valuable things in my life can never be reduced to numbers or statistics and can never be bought or sold, and Alyssa knew this too.

At the end of the day what is really important in life is family, friends, and leaving this Earth better than we found it. The right degree usually increases your job options, starting a business is fulfilling, and of course, being rich and famous is every middle school student's dream. However, after much world travel and a few orbits of the sun, I have seen some really stressed rich yuppies and some really relaxed poor folk in my life. I teach kids to aim high, to set goals, and to work hard, but I always remind them that finding peace in nature, feeling solace in your relations, and serving others is the best reward. Money cannot buy laughter, true friendship, or the fulfillment of a job well done. Too many kids believe the hype of material happiness, and this leads to disappointment and even violence.

17

⌒

CUT TO THE BONE

The fight is never about grapes or lettuce. It is always about people.

Cesar Chavez

I let the kids go a couple of minutes early to let them out in the sunshine but heard some put-downs outside the door, so I stepped out. Alyssa and Skyler were sitting on the step outside the front doors of our portable, and Skyler was coloring blood-red onto rags around his wrists, feigning suicide I assumed. Most of the kids were asking why he was doing that and remarking about how "gay" it was and "retarded," and other adolescent terms for confusion and difference. Skyler ignored a lot but occasionally responded with a "Shut the f—k up" and "Mind your f—king business." In retrospect, I should have done more, but I simply made the harassers move to their next class, and I asked Alyssa and Skyler to go in the bathroom, clean up, and go to their next class too. I stepped back into my classroom, and within about thirty seconds, I heard sounds of a fight.

Alyssa liked to dress in black and paint her eyes like a weeping heroin junkie vampire. She drew dragons and manga raccoons and was a quiet, shy, sweetheart, but she had gone ballistic on the harassing bullies. The girlfriend of one of the bullies jumped in to pull Alyssa off. Then Skyler joined in, and the main bully clocked Skyler in the jaw. You would need a diagram to understand fully the chaos. At this point, I came outside to restrain Makayla from beating Skyler, who was bleeding from the mouth, and then tried to assess the damage.

The main bully had been in three fights that year, was popular and cute, and said he was "cut to the bone." I did not believe him, so he showed me the white bone and pulsating muscle, veins, and other signs of serious injury. He claimed it was because Alyssa threw him to the ground, but witnesses confirmed it was because of his blindsided punch to Skyler's mouth that sent Skyler's two front teeth flying. The bully got what he deserved. He ended up in the hospital and kicked out of school for mistaking anger for strength. I have no patience for bullies.

Poor Skyler had just had his front teeth fixed with caps the day before and now was toothless again. The details of the consequences are only interesting to fellow teachers, but the backgrounds of the kids involved included physical, emotional, and sexual abuse, neglect, suicide in the family, and obvious anger-management issues. I will never forget Alyssa's quivering voice on the phone that night when I called her from my home and helped her process the event. I will always remember the ghostly white of the bully's self-exposed knucklebone. In contrast, when I was punched in college for the first time, I told the guy that I forgave him—then he tried to punch me again.

That is the problem with confirmation bias, we all tend to think we are right, then find evidence to support our belief system. That is the value of teaching the scientific method, but also learning the intuition of the heart. The mind can so easily justify, rationalize, and dogmatize our thoughts, that our actions are just self-fulfilling prophecies. We carry all that baggage of our own childhoods with our preconceived ideas based on our small set of experiences, which are often very different than our students.

18

Fart Girls

You had an arse full of farts that night, darling...

James Joyce

Weston had a childhood history of sexual abuse that twisted his views of sexuality toward the strange and sometimes macabre. We, and the other students, caught him three times last year looking at pornography on the Internet during class and lunchtime with a room full of witnesses. He ruined his reputation in the school, so we thought this year might be different if we used a little preventative mentoring. I pulled him aside and told him I would trust him in my class to use the Internet for research, and that smart, nice kids like him would eventually find love and affection from girls, but that acting like a "creep" would leave him lonely forever. I explained our common experiences with temptation, pornography, and finding inner strength and reminded him that no Internet filter or set of consequences would be more powerful than his own conscience. I thought it was a powerful and salient talk, as do most adults on their high horse.

Despite my attempts, the next week I caught him looking on Google Video for "fart girls." His search terms included "fart," "girls," "naked," and "porno." The poor kid was so technologically ignorant that he did not even bother erasing his "history" toolbar, and even if he was not caught hairy-handed, anyone could look up his searches with the touch of a button. After discussing this with his caseworker, I read his file about his difficulties at other schools. He had often been made fun of for his quirks, and despite having strong academic skills, he had the social skills of a fourth grader.

Weston was expelled from his last school after stabbing a harassing student with a pencil. He had been made fun of for a whole class period. Then he reported hearing a humming noise in his head before entering a trancelike state in which he claimed a loss of control over his actions. After the stabbing incident and returning to his Earth mind, he realized that the humming noise was actually himself, humming away while he avenged his tormentor. Reading his history was disturbing yet enlightening, both to see how far he had come at our school and how much further he had to go. Someday I hoped he would look back on the kind words of someone who helped him to kick his porno habits and find value in his strengths. Either that or he would be remembering the words of a judge handing down his sentence.

1 9

⌒

WAY TOO EASY

The biggest human temptation is to settle for too little.

Thomas Merton

Everyone faces temptation in life, and while my British side says, "Locked doors only keep out honest men," my Persian side says, "Trust in Allah, but always tie up your camel." My mom said to trust people until they prove themselves untrustworthy, but my dad said to trust only those who earn your trust. Of course, business is different from teaching, and friendships are different from students, so I try not to overgeneralize. When deciding how much to trust someone, I often use a combination of prior experience, intuition, and reading body language. This is essential for a teacher, since we often have to make judgment calls about kids' honesty. Having an intuitive moral compass allows one to examine one's own intent and actions, admit mistakes, and avoid the myriad of temptations of modern life. I often have to make amends, admit my faults, and discern correct action.

Most kids today are so bombarded by distracting temptations that choosing a healthy lifestyle requires strong parenting and community support. It is just too easy today for kids to get their hands on alcohol, drugs, pornography, gratuitous media violence, and weapons. I am a firm believer in the Bill of Rights and do not see this as primarily a legislative problem. While a little more gun control, like mandatory background checks, even at gun shows, or banning certain assault weapons, would probably help reduce school violence, it is oversimplifying the issue to legislate morality. While stronger spam- and pop-up-related laws could limit erotic advertising, it is a violation of free speech if taken too far. Our children, however, have a right to not have their childhood innocence scarred by images of sex and violence.

There were at least three adults charged with encouraging child abuse in our little idyllic town of Waldorf schools and aikido dojos. Two of the offenders were middle-aged members of prominent local families whose parents were respected community members. It seems that even when you try to do everything right, kids can still grow up to be psychotic, neurotic, pornographic, or subject to addiction. These issues have always been around, and all of my friends remember the first time they were shown a *Playboy* or *Hustler* magazine. We usually had to make an effort to find pornography, borrowing from a weird dad or uncle's stash or shamefully trying to buy it at the store. Either prospect was degrading and, frankly, gross if you really thought about why your friend's dad's magazine was so worn out.

These days such natural aversions are avoided by the simple clicking of a mouse or the typing of a curious search term on the Internet. As a teacher, I have had to deal with this case so many times that it is truly sad. How to handle pornography, trolls, and predators is now a necessary precautionary lesson before allowing any Internet access to children of any age. Despite filtering technology, I have had to teach kids what to do when any image comes up that makes them feel uncomfortable. I have taught kids never to give out any true personal information online and never to believe who someone says they are on the Internet.

I have run e-mail pen pals across the world and never had a problem, but I have had pornography pop-ups come up at a summer-camp computer lab, and I had to jump across the room and turn the screen off before some little third grader's image of women was permanently stained. I have had to remove Internet privileges from a student who simply typed in "breast" and was overwhelmed with the resulting images. I teach kids that their heart is their best filter, and that if something feels wrong, it probably is wrong.

This is what makes the ease of Internet pornography so dangerous. In this voyeuristic age of *Jackass* and YouTube, what starts as childhood curiosity can devolve into morbid curiosity. The sick people who were arrested in my town did not start out watching child rape, but through systematic desensitization, they had lost all sense of intuitive morality. This is not about our loss of religious direction, since members of every faith from Catholic to Muslim have been involved in terrible cases of abuse. As with other moral issues, we have faced these, too, since time immemorial, but the ease of access to pornography today tempts even an honest man. I am not saying I miss the innocent days of my uncle's dog-eared *Playboys*, but I know that kids today face much harder and deadlier temptations whose accessibility is excessively easy.

2 0

⌒

LYING TO A THIEF

A lie told often enough becomes the truth.

Vladimir Lenin

*L*ying to teachers was excessively easy for Jacob, even easier than stealing. He was the same student who was expelled for one year for getting into three fights. Then he was involved in a wallet theft the year after. Of course, he completely denied it and even tried to finger another student, claiming he had seen the kid fumbling through the wallet and throwing something in the bushes. We tried everything we could, including searching the new student who was accused, but we came up empty-handed.

The new student, Blade, also claimed total innocence, but he let us search him anyway. I had to call his dad and let him know our suspicions. Blade's dad was understandably upset that I had "accused" his son, but I tried to explain that we just wanted him to be aware of the situation and to keep an eye out for sudden wads of cash or new expensive items. The hundred dollars stolen was a kid's rent money, and although it was foolish to leave that kind of cash in an unguarded wallet, we all empathized with the loss.

I decided to try my good cop/bad cop approach and took Jacob aside at the bus stop. I told him that I wanted to be able to trust my students, to leave my cell phone on my desk, to lend out headphones, and to have a school where we felt safe. I told him that if he could get back the money, I would say nothing and ask no questions. His eye started to twitch as he tried to look me in the eye and lie about his lack of involvement, and yet revealed his good intentions to "see what he could do" to get the money back. I actually intended to trick the petty thief into getting it back, then turn around and confront the facts with the police involved. When I told the veteran teachers what I had done, they were in shock. They said that I would ruin any trust in adults that he had. I would just be another adult who had betrayed him, so I decided to honor my word and not lie to a known thief and bully.

The veteran teachers were openly shocked at my approach and recommended I not use it in the future. Ironically, the next day Jacob came and asked to speak to me in private. He brought me fifty dollars, claiming he got it from a kid at the bus transfer station. Of course, we all knew the truth—that he and Blade had split the winnings, and that my guilt trip had only worked on one of them. Jacob said he would do his best to get the other half back but made no guarantees. Within fifteen minutes, Blade approached me, asking if I had gotten some of the stolen loot back and saying he would help Jacob to get the rest from the culprit. Of course, I knew he was lying and could tell he was probably just going to keep it anyway.

His father came in that same morning, and as I introduced myself, I held out my hand, only to be left hanging by the ingrate. Despite my best efforts to be polite and contrite, he was rude and offended that his son was being "accused." His first words upon entering the main office were, "Well, I have got myself an attorney if you want to take this to the police." We were apologetic and tried to explain that, since Blade was the only one seen with the wallet, we had to search him, but had no intent to press charges, involve the police, or require further action from parents or attorneys. I wanted to tell him we were pretty darn sure that his son had been part of the theft, but instead we just tried to quell his obvious pent-up anger.

It was no wonder the kid was in such deep denial when his father worked so hard to cover up for him. I did not know if the dad really believed what he was saying, or if he just lived so deeply in denial that he did not recognize his own reflection in his son (whom he named

Blade!). I have known some Aura Sunshine Rainbows in my life, but I have to wonder what significance the name Blade holds for his father.

I felt proud that Jacob trusted me enough to return the money, and the other teachers said this was the first time they had ever seen such an approach work. I was amazed that he did the right thing for no other reason than his conscience, since he could have just as easily kept the booty without consequence. I hoped that we could get the other half back too, but since we did not, I took this small victory as a sign that change was possible.

I often wear my heart on my sleeve and am very open with students about my own challenges in life. I know they say not to be friends with your students, but that does not preclude being friendly, honest, and real as an influential adult and mentor in their lives. I believe that teaching is really soul work and that, when done correctly, teachers and students connect on a much deeper level than merely subject matter being taught. Of course, in this case, this meant I could not lie, even to a thief. Seeing teaching as soul work might sound antithetical to my scientific pedagogy, but I am always surprised by how many teachers see this job as a spiritual calling.

21

JEWS IN HEAVEN

I think that the roots of racism have always been econom-ic, and I think people are desperate and scared. And when you're desperate and scared you scapegoat people. It exac-erbates latent tendencies toward—well, toward racism or homophobia or anti-Semitism.

Henry Louis Gates

Sometimes it seems like most Oregonians believe that the Earth will end in Armageddon, and in Phoenix, Oregon, it is a common belief. I had a student who agreed with former President George W. Bush that there is one right religion in the world and it will conquer all other religions in a grand heavenly battle. I asked him if he found it at all disturbing that the commander in chief, with access to "nukyular" weapons, wants the world to end in an apocalyptic battle between re-ligions, where only one comes out on top, and he replied, "Well, there will probably be some Jews in heaven too." I asked him about the bil-lion or so Chinese and Indians who followed other religions, and his response was, "God will decide who lives and who dies, and he'll prob-ably let some Chinese live too." It does not seem very spiritual if only they are right and the majority of the world is wrong. Of course, I am just as guilty because I think I am right that we should accept others no matter what their belief system, and that the fruits of our actions are more important than which prophet we follow.

I am still surprised by how many rational, intelligent Oregonians believe we are living in the End Times. We survived Y2K, the 2012 Mayan calendar hype, and even fires, floods, and recessions, but for some godforsaken reason, many Christians still await the Rapture of the Book of Revelation any day. We were discussing it in our faculty lunchroom one day, and the librarian and three teacher's aides all thought the signs were clear. I really get along with most of them, and we agree on most aspects of education, but that's why it is best to not discuss sex, religion, or politics in the lunchroom. We have stressful enough jobs without bringing debate into our digestive chambers, but sometimes it just comes up, and I am shocked. Maybe it is my multicultural atheist background, but it seems so parochial and petty to assume that your path to God is the only one, and that all others are going to suffer for eternity.

I am dogmatic in my relativism. The only absolute truth is that truth is relative. But if that's true, then I must accept that others can believe what they want, even if it means self-fulfilling Armageddon for us all. I respect their beliefs, even if I think they are wrong. I certainly would not tell anyone what God says, or that one book is God's word, but if I am truly open-minded, I must be willing to see that they might be on the one true path, and that all others are led astray, including myself. Unfortunately, I have lived enough to see that religion is less important than just being kind, and as Jesus said, the whole of the law can be summed up by "let your yes be yes, and your no be no." I hope that is the main ticket to heaven, but even if not, it sure is a healthy way to live life with integrity, Jewish or Moorish. Opening people's minds to multicultural belief systems comes in many forms. There is no need to mention God, Allah, Buddha, or Krishna to teach spiritual values. Sometimes it can be as down to earth as simply sharing a meal.

22

~

Supervised Lunch

To lengthen thy life, lessen thy meals.

Benjamin Franklin

Often when I had lunch duty, I did not even get a five-minute break from 8:00 a.m. to 5:00 p.m. It was predictable irony when I would finally sit down to eat my sandwich in the school's main room, where kids ate and hung out. I needed to supervise them, but a few lonely boys always supervised me. You have to realize that many had never met their father, and others wished they never had.

As I sat there with mustard and tomato drippings on my chin, a kid with mild autism kept asking me if I would like to travel to another planet. Of course, my mouth was totally full, as I had only ten minutes to eat, spending the rest of my lunch checking kids off lists, changing kids' schedules, and resolving petty disturbances. I tried to answer in between bites, and even moved my seat a couple of times, hoping he would get the hint. But he just kept on talking while I chewed and then longingly awaited my response with bated breath. I explained that we have not even explored the bottom of the sea or discovered every animal in the rainforest, so I had no need for interplanetary travel.

Since this did not quench his thirst for attention, I was forced to go to the bathroom in search of a paper towel to wipe my messy mouth. He and his little buddy actually followed me to the bathroom door, and after I wiped my mouth, I decided to lock myself in and relieve myself just to get a break. I then took ten deep breaths in a stinky middle-school toilet, just so I could find some shelter from the storm. I thought that maybe a little judicious stalling in the stall would lose my new admirers, but they waited like lost puppies until I came back out and then continued the conversation like nothing had happened.

I accommodated their queries for as long as I could and then made an excuse to go into the office to print a student's report card. I felt like crying when I thought about how much these kids were crying out for some male attention, so much so that they would stand over a messy tofu-sandwich-eating teacher and wait outside a bathroom stall, just to have a little positive feedback. Although I felt exhausted and stressed out for not getting my needed five-minute break, I was glad that they felt comfortable enough with me to ruin my lunch, saving them from their solitude. There was much more at stake than my lunch break.

23

Hamburger Meat

Your fears are not walls, but hurdles. Courage is not the absence of fear, but the conquering of it.

Dan Millman

𝓑e forewarned that this story is probably the most disturbing that I have ever heard, but gives insight into the world in which these kids are thrown. I was holding a baby girl during night school, as our parent-teacher conferences entailed a fourteen-hour day, 8:00 a.m. until 10:00 p.m. at night. I had a break in the conferences, and the baby girl, Melissa, was fussing and distracting her babysitting GED student from her work, so I offered to help. I was glad to have the chance to show them a caring male role model and to give myself a break from the complicated drama of underserved students. As my break time ended, I handed her back to her babysitter, who told me why the state had taken her friend's baby.

The birthmother would routinely use a pillow over the baby's face to stifle her cries and had told the babysitter that she hated her own child. I certainly could not have been a patient parent at seventeen, but I hope I would not have had such malice toward my own flesh and blood. The culminating event was the birthparents buying a pet rat and keeping it in the same room as the baby with the cage uncovered. For whatever reason, they left the baby unattended for several hours with the pillow over her head, not knowing that the rat had gotten out and was hungry. I can barely even write these words, but by the time the ambulance arrived, the poor baby girl's arm and the back of her neck "looked like hamburger meat," as the student described it. These are details I could not make up, would never imagine, and haunted my dreams and my waking hours with my own children. College had not prepared me to handle this aspect of education.

Of course, the parents were arrested for neglect, the baby was sent to a foster home, and she was now being babysat by a couple of eighteen-year-old dropouts. I want to believe in a just universe, but my wife and I had four miscarriages, had to wait over four years, before finally being blessed with a two-month-premature son, yet rat-owning, pillow-stifling dropouts seem to procreate like vermin. I still try to teach them to be better people, even if I sometimes lean toward forced sterilization. I know this sounds terrible, though, and I would never give the state that power, given that they already control our urination.

After the conferences ended, and on my drive home, I saw one of the babysitters sitting on the curb, holding a cigarette in one hand and the divine infant in the other. I did not have the patience left to stop and tell her she was violating school smoking policy and endangering the baby with secondhand smoke. I had to choose my battles and save my strength for the ongoing struggle against ignorance. This is our job as teachers, for we are peaceful warriors in a world of senseless aggression.

I hesitate to call it a divine mission or a spiritual calling, but I know that the best teachers have a living passion that is not easily fazed by worldly woes. Of course, we all have bad days, days when we question our jobs or the impossibility of reaching certain kids, but to stay strong in this profession requires a deeper connection to some higher purpose. We certainly cannot be motivated by money or power, for that leads too quickly to administration, professorship, or policy lobbying. We need all those people, and I appreciate a servant leader as much as anyone, but to be a classroom teacher, you have to love working with kids.

Of course, some kids have very challenging and annoying behaviors; that is undeniable. To love that child unconditionally, as much even as the teacher's pet, is one of the hardest parts of this job. It is much easier when they are younger and less responsible for their situations, but I struggle to keep my hope alive when high-school kids continue to repeat the patterns of their dysfunctional families. I have to remember what they looked like when they were first born, when they first looked into their mother's eyes. Then I remember that they deserve love like anyone, maybe even more. So I take a deep breath and try again. As teachers we never know which comment, which action will have meaning for a student, but sometimes the results of a generous action are pain and punishment.

24

ASSAULT FOR A SWEATER

If everyone demanded peace instead of another television set, then there'd be peace.

John Lennon

We were going to give away the lost-and-found items to Goodwill anyway, so we decided to let the kids claim any items that had been lost. After that, we let them just pick out items they wanted instead of buying them from Goodwill. That was the first mistake, setting the dominoes in a downward spiral. The shy, quiet, dragon-drawing Christin chose a Marilyn Manson sweater, which three months later was claimed by a truant student. But Christin refused to return the sweater, and a teacher did not handle the issue promptly enough, so the truant student's sister decided to take it back by force one day after school.

Shy, gothic Christin returned to school with her black eyeliner running down her face like Tammy Faye Bakker, except with scratches and bruises all over her arms. She had been "jumped" by at least three other girls who held her to the ground and beat her until another gothic boy saved her from a probable hospital visit. Of the three assailants, one was a known Norteño gang member and two had been sexually abused and were living with adoptive parents. They were under investigation for assault and theft—all because they lacked the patience and foresight to get the sweater back through mature means.

I held it together emotionally, but inside wanted to tell those weak cowards what I really thought about them ganging up on a shy, quiet, and kind artist. Just another day at the office, but I was not too jaded to cry on my drive home. I said a prayer and promised myself I would not let joking threats, MTV-generation put-downs, or ancient adolescent fake bravado slide in my classroom anymore. We all used insults to feign strength in our youth, but in these Columbine days of nightly cage fights at the county fairgrounds, words can come back to haunt us. School violence is a real reflection of a violent world.

When I was a kid, we hid under our desks and prepared for the Russians starting a nuclear holocaust, but now kids hide in dark corners, pretending a mass shooter is knocking at the door, even in first grade. It is terrifying, painfully Orwellian, and confusing for a teacher on how to impart the import of the drill without giving kids nightmares about school safety. I never felt safer after our "fallout" drills, and I mostly remember them as fun. I whisper stories to the kids while we wait in unlit corners, out of view of any window, silently awaiting the "all clear" signal to return to normal.

If this is normal, then I am proud to be weird. I still think teachers can change this world, but pedaling uphill gets tiring. Fitting into a sick society does not make one well. The schools and this country are filled with hardworking, intelligent, and caring individuals, yet mainstream society cannot agree on the cause of our sickness. Fundamentally, I still believe that the political system and consumer culture need to change, but that change has to start within ourselves first. As long as our society values money over people, short-term gain over longevity, and cheap plastic toys over nature, then I will be a subtle subversive and an educational revolutionary. I will teach by any means necessary.

25

THE NUMBER XIV

*Hip-hop is supposed to uplift and create, to educate people
on a larger level, and to make a change.*

Doug E. Fresh

We arrived at school one Monday to find an elaborate display of rocks spelling out "Tiny" and "XIV," but we just thought it was the work of a wannabe gang member. Not knowing the significance of the number fourteen, we Googled it to find it stood for the letter *N*, the tag of the Norteño gang. Just one week earlier, three students had jumped Christin over a sweater, and the main assailant, Martina, was lodged for assault and theft. Of course, like many of our students, she had a previous record, and because of Measure 11, mandatory minimums, she was sentenced to six years for a sweater.

Once lodged, she began to send threats to the victims through her friends, saying how they should stab the main victim and whoever called the cops. Of course, I had called the police when I saw the bruised and bleeding victim return to school in tears. I was not a big fan of the "Five-O" and only involved them in such extreme cases, but to think that doing the right thing resulted in death threats was sad and scary.

Then, we found out that Martina was claiming to be a gang member straight out of Mexico. She wrote a fantasy piece about being "jumped in" by her "street family" in Mexico and how her "homies" were glad she was moving to America so she could recruit more members. The only problem was she was not a gang member, she was born in the United States, and she never even lived in Mexico. She wanted respect from her classmates and thought that faking gang membership would fit right into the MTV generation of *Yo Momma*–loving hip-hop confusion.

From the wife-beater tank tops to the cheap and cheesy gold chains and fake ghetto lingo, she had all her peers fooled. The police told us that wannabe gang members are much more dangerous than real ones, since they will do anything to become a real gang member, or at least to convince others they are genuine in something. This seventeen-year-old girl with a sweet smile tagged, threatened, and assaulted her way into six years of wasted time doing real lockup to get fake respect.

The gang culture of pimps and ho's, rollin' on dubs and poppin' collars, is so prevalent in the trailer parks that it is a multicultural phenomenon. The Aryan Nation, Norteños, Bloods and Crips should just get together and compare their sagging pants to realize that they have all missed the real hip-hop boat. Despite falling for the trappings of hip-hop music and material bling, they neglect the original elements. Break dancing, graffiti, lyricism, and turntablism are the fundamental aspects of hip-hop, not the empty swagger of saggy pants.

I have seen so much attitude change come from educating youths about the positive aspects of hip-hop culture; when given an outlet, their talents shine. I have seen kids make multitracked beats with rhymes about their struggles in school, their multicultural roots, their hunger at night, and how they will grow up to be an astronaut. I have seen music, dance, and the arts transform kids, teaching them how to code-switch, or seamlessly alternate between their street culture and academic culture. By valuing what kids like and then finding ways to educate them about the positive aspects of their interests, a teacher can make compost from manure.

Of course, single isolated teachers cannot break down gang culture by themselves, but there are proven programs that empower kids through opportunity. I have seen third-generation Norteños break the cycle and be the first in their family history to attend college. I have also lost far too many to the streets, the prison-industrial complex, or an early grave. There is no simple equation, but strong parents, schools, and community support systems are essential variables. Alternative, charter, and magnet schools provide needed choices for diverse learners, yet for some, only residential treatment or removal from the home is the best option.

26

A STEP ABOVE THE GUTTER

We are all in the gutter, but some of us are looking at the stars.

Oscar Wilde

The twenty-five-year veteran teachers at this charter school hated to let a kid go because they knew that if they could not make it in our preventative program, they would probably end up on the streets. Being a charter school is not supposed to make you an alternative school or a school for dropouts, but that became our reality. The rest of the mainstream schools in our district did not really serve these kids, and they were quick to suspend, expel, or send them to residential treatment programs if they were lucky. I remember the first kid sent into residential treatment and how the veterans told me it was his best chance for getting out of an abusive home. Once they hit eighteen, the only program the state offers is prison, where they are warehoused and schooled in true street knowledge, from which few return to any sort of meaningful rehabilitation.

That is why we gave these kids five last chances, why we hated to refer them back to their home-district schools, and why we spent 90 percent of our time dealing with 10 percent of our students, or those who were the most at risk. It was a formula for teacher burnout, scaring away homeschoolers and TAG kids, and initiating more drug abuse, theft, and school violence. Ideally, the mainstream schools would provide services for this needy population, but because of the funding criteria of George W. Bush's "No Child Left Behind," their state test scores were better off by separating the wheat from the chaff. Our program faced the same choice, between serving kids or looking good for state tests, and despite the federal government's economic threats, we taught kids rather than tests.

Since leaving that position and after several scathing newspaper articles about how our program was "bringing down" the district scores, the charter school dropped its GED program. They kept the night school for kids doing credit retrieval, but since a GED counts for nothing on state and national standards, most students who had full-time jobs simply dropped out of school to make ends meet. Of course, it was not their fault for needing a full-time job to feed, clothe, and keep a roof over their heads, but at age sixteen, it must be hard to see the value of staying in school to get a degree when no one provides for your basic needs.

I do not know the best solution, but I know that many of the GED students learned a lot more and worked a lot harder than kids who do the seat time and get D's in order to get a "real" diploma. The GED tests actually required demonstration of knowledge, and I had real respect for the farmers, ranchers, timber workers, and fast-food workers who showed up when I was going home. While many used the GED program as an easy out instead of completing their high-school credits, quite a few were stuck between choosing homelessness or school. They did not want to work a full-time job and go to school, but you do not always get what you want.

Sometimes you do not even get what you need; though as I was taught, you always get the experience you need and you create your own reality. This is easy to say as a child of privilege or a new-age mantra, but the harsh reality is far from this idyllic vision. If having a GED and a full-time job keeps kids a step above the gutter, then I honor their tenacity, even if the state counts it as failing.

27

NO CHILD LEFT STANDING

Learning happens in the minds and souls, not in the data-bases of multiple-choice tests.

Ken Robinson

George W. Bush believed that all students should be held to the same standard. Of course, this meant a kid from a trailer park with autism, Tourette's syndrome, and ADHD had to pass the same standardized test as a talented-and-gifted kid from a mansion in the hills. Not only must such students pass the same test, but they were allowed no modifications except extended testing time, the questions being read to them aloud, and larger fonts. G. W. Bush said that he believed all kids could succeed, but then if a school's state test scores did not go up every year, that school was labeled "unacceptable" and risked losing federal funding.

Ironically, the struggling students in the lowest-funded school districts received less money for performing badly just one week out of the entire school year. If this "unacceptable" status continued for three years, they were considered "failing" and could have all their faculty fired, new administrators hired, and even vouchers given to parents for private "choice" schools. It was really an underhanded plan to bankrupt the public school system and privatize education for the privileged in G. W.'s new "ownership" society.

The icing on the cake was that school growth was measured not by a student's growth from one year to the next, but by comparing the current year's tenth graders to last year's. It is far too complicated in this space-age, Internet-driven society to measure each student's real growth, so we use aggregate data from year to year to determine a school's growth over time. God forbid we have a sudden influx of second-language learners or teach in a small school with only 10 eighth graders, because then that so-called statistically significant data would be used to cut our nose to spite our face. G. W.'s plan did not care if you moved to the United States just two months ago or were a schizophrenic dyslexic. He would not allow any child to be left behind, even if it meant eliminating band, art, and elementary librarians from most schools—all in order to meet an elitist capitalist agenda.

I am sure it is not intentional, and that those espousing such methods are not evil people; they just believe that the private sector can do a better job than government. Being a biodiesel business owner, often paying more money in fuel taxes than made in net profits, I fully understand the aversion to government programs. I think government should be involved only in projects for the common good and in which the profit motive would interfere with best practices. The list includes education, health care, libraries, public transportation, and infrastructure, not to mention public safety and international relations.

I know I cannot solve all the world's problems, but I've always thought quality education was a logical place to start. Paying teachers more than plumbers might attract the best and brightest, not just the bleeding-heart, overgenerous workaholics. I have seen a few slacker teachers in my time, but the vast majority is so overwhelmingly dedicated; it is part of who they are.

Dedication cannot compensate for overcrowding two sets of twenty-five kindergarteners into the same classroom for half-day sessions with one teacher. The poor teacher did not even have enough cubbies for the students, who had to share cubbies, then was tasked with cleaning them out every day so the afternoon groups could share them again. It cannot be best practices to pack forty-two kids into a middle-school math or science class or over a hundred kids onto a special education teacher's caseload. Whether it is Bush's "No Child Left Behind," Obama's "Race to the Top," or any other slogan, what works is honoring the multiple intelligences that make us human, keeping class sizes to a minimum, and valuing the profession that educates the next generation.

It is no wonder that many veteran teachers become wary of the latest fashion in educational innovation, since Obama's Smarter Balanced testing and Common Core standards are not that different from the Oaks tests and state standards—just more and more complicated, tedious, and time-consuming. We have students taking these tests three times, in some cases to try to move from "meeting" to "exceeding" the standard, and definitely taking it three times to move up from the "not meeting" level. I also know there are best practices and models to turn even the poorest, most neglected students into college-bound intellectuals, but they all require more time, money, and priority on quality teaching. Parental support is a key component of these programs, but once again, the method of measurement determines the emphasis. Even the Harlem Academy lacks a focus on music and art, but it consistently scores above the 75th percentile on standardized tests. Performance data has many interpolations, but a computer can never judge a piano recital, an oral report on local history, or a lesson that changes a kid's thoughts about life.

I have seen so many students brought to tears on test day, so many students' self-esteem damaged by thinking they were dumb, and very few truly helped by the emphasis on high-stakes testing. We now even pull kindergarteners out of class if they do not meet an arbitrary standard, one that ignores individual developmental differences. We stigmatize and ostracize, we test and retest, and we remediate and segregate, all in the name of keeping up with China.

I had a brilliant son of a fellow teacher who was convinced he was dumb because he could not reach the DIBELS reading benchmark of eighty-five words per minute. Yet when given the chance to demonstrate knowledge in a wholistic project, he could memorize and recite details ad infinitum. He definitely read more slowly than the average, but he retained much more, picked up way more details, and made generalizing connections unmeasured on the DIBELS scale. Of course, we have to catch kids that are missing core concepts or falling further and further behind the curve, but we should still honor multiple intelligences and multimodal demonstrations of knowledge.

Teachers use the best kinds of testing on a daily, weekly, and monthly basis to evaluate student learning, and then they reteach any concepts missed in an individualized or group setting.

All master teachers use this ongoing performance assessment. They never assume that just because they taught it, all the students really learned it. It is always surprising when, after a month of hands-on, project-based lessons on a topic, there remain several students unable to demonstrate a simple definition on a written test, although those students could give countless examples of the concept in action. I have had many students who could give me three examples of mitigation projects that we did, but could not define "mitigation." As a self-reflective teacher, I find this is invaluable information that will direct future lessons. This attention is what helps children to not get left behind, and it helps teachers stand firmly in the knowledge of what students really know without teaching to the test. Caring teachers know their students more intimately than a number on a screen.

2 8

 .·—

ALL IN THE FAMILY

Behind every person who's committed an unimaginable crime is an adult who committed unimaginable violence against them as a child.

Ji-young Gong

*M*ary had been missing my first-period math class a lot, but she had written an amazing poem in audio technology. She refused to record the piece in front of others, taking the microphone out the back door of the classroom, but even then still whispering so no one would hear. It was all about Mary's father dying, and it described how her mother was spending the insurance money on a revolving cycle of boyfriends. She described the abusive excuses for stepfathers—and worst of all, uncles—who had violated her sanctity. It was hard to read without crying, but hearing her fiery whisper, a mélange of intense sadness and rage, really brought tears to my eyes.

Soon after, she could not really function at all in class and kept saying she needed to talk to someone. I finally found a female teacher who had a prep period, who later told me the sordid details. She was experiencing incontinence and had a bladder and urinary tract infection because of intense sexual abuse at home. I asked what I could do, and she said to just be very sensitive to her need to go to the bathroom. Apparently, incontinence was a side effect of her abuse, and I do not even want to imagine how or why. We have to report such incidents to the Department of Child Protective Services by law, yet nothing will ever replace her lost innocence. Could a standardized test really do justice to her plight?

In another case, Ethan's mom tried everything to help her son with mild autism to succeed in school and life. She served on the school board and the budget committee and volunteered in the classroom. Ethan was doing better in school, but had never quite fit in socially because of his acne, glasses, high-pitched voice, and lack of social graces and attention to social cues. He was a very nice and intelligent young man when he applied himself, and with his mom delivering stern and consistent routines, he was learning to just get by. I did a mediation between him and an equally challenged OCD Hispanic boy who was recovering from abuse. Learning to get those two guys to agree on anything was a real learning process for me, and I thank the master teacher who taught me the method. People really can change, especially kids. Sometimes it takes just one person at the right time to help them change their lives forever. I still believe it because I have seen it so many times.

Computer testing cannot capture these life lessons, nor can statistics measure them—policy wonks will never fully understand them. They make a classroom like an extended family, often teaching the communication tools and values that are absent at home, or reinforcing what parents have tried so hard to instill in their children. They are stories that I would never have imagined until they happened, with details that I could never make up. While some teachers are content just to teach social studies or math, I will always try to see each child, no matter how annoying or challenging, as an innocent baby, as part of my family. I do not always succeed, but I make a habit of trying.

29

⌒

VIDIOTS

Video games offer violent messages, and even the sports
video games include taunting and teasing.

Geoffrey Canada

I always tell kids that if they spent two hours a day watching
TV or playing video games, that would add up to about 10 percent of their life; meaning, every ten years they will have spent a full
year zoned out. Imagine a full year learning a foreign language, pro-
gramming a computer, writing a book, or just doing something other
than brain-candy mental masturbation. The kids never reacted with a
grand revelation or seemed that shocked, but I always hoped it might
be like a seed planted in dry ground, which when moistened by time
and experience would sprout into a new way of life.

I never know what the fruits of my actions will produce, and I am
quickly learning to let go of the consequences. I am a wandering tree
planter, planting seeds of self-realization, and never knowing whether
those trees will wither and die or thrive and spread fruit in due season.
There's an old saying about planting trees under whose shade we will
never sit, and taking nothing personally is a prerequisite. Of course, I
would never want to end up like some teachers, who rarely show any
emotion except stress and seem completely insensitive to the kids

around them. We all have those days, but some make it their general demeanor.

I may end up the same after thirty years of teaching, but with almost twenty classroom years under my belt, I still get teary-eyed in front of the kids when something deeply affects me. I can choke up over a classic song we sing, a powerful performance, or a breakthrough moment in a class meeting. I am much more reticent in expressing anger, although I have told a student he needed to keep his mouth closed or I would kick him out of my class. I was not feeling well myself, and this was a clear lack of self-discipline on my part because just as I was trained, I have a clear system of consequences. I try not to make exceptions when I really like a kid, because I usually end up feeling frustrated when I give someone too many chances and then finally lose my temper. I would rather that a child lose fifteen minutes of class time than that I lose my temper.

Being centered as a teacher is crucial to quality instruction. A teacher who is tired, hungover, upset, stressed out, or sick usually struggles to maintain the energy and patience necessary to orchestrate a classroom. I have tried to teach under all of the above conditions and can attest to the ill effects. The older I have gotten, the more important eight hours of sleep, regular exercise, a healthy social life, and a regular meditation practice have become. I have also realized that most of my stress comes from things in the past or the future, and that the more present I am, the more life seems to work out. It is not that life gets easier when I relax, but that I take it easier on others and myself. My family appreciates this centeredness, which I cannot acquire from video games, television, computers, or any other screen time. I love all these devices, but I do not want to spend more time on them than reading, making music or art, exercising, or playing with my own kids. Minutes add up to hours, then days, then years wasted.

Our digital devices have become so ingrained, and apparently innocuous, yet they dominate our consciousness. It is so hard for children's young brains to maintain focus and imagination when force-fed digital media. I am not a Luddite, but I have seen myself and my own children subtly slip into passive acceptance, then active participation in the madness of modernity. Even people who can barely fill out an online form feel obliged to return a text when out to dinner. My best friend does not even own a cell phone, but wants instant answers to minutia when the Internet is available. We become so accustomed to instant gratification and short attention spans that information entitlement follows suit.

It is much harder to wait, to look it up in a book, or to stay on task for a whole hour when our devices beckon us with blips, beeps, and vibrations. Unfortunately, attention is a learned behavior, and the more we let devices distract from and dictate our reality, the less able we are to discern what is truly important in life. The first time I played *Space Invaders* on Atari as a kid, I would see pulsating aliens on the back of my eyelids at night, and even so-called educational games can turn avid readers into vidiots.

I am not about to say that no one should ever play a video game; after all, many people use them as a healthy outlet for relaxation. I do know that among the thousands of students that I have taught though, the more screen time they get, the less physically active they are, the less curiosity they possess, and the shorter the attention span they have. I also know that the younger these technologies are introduced, the worse the impact on developing brains. Research and endless anecdotal evidence supports this, despite the industry's push for "smart" technologies for babies. The world is always changing, but some habits are hard to break.

30

⌒

YOU ARE SO GAY

I always say that as a Christian I cannot find any passage in the Gospels in which Jesus condemned homosexuality.

Troy Perry

I still use the word "awesome," have stopped using "rad," and try to stay hip to the latest chillaxing, hyphy vocabulary. I frequently show my age and feel quite old in my hippie B-boy steez, but some phrases have not changed in twenty years. It is still the most common daily put-down to call someone "gay." An activity or decision students do not like is "so gay," and a homosexual is still a "fag." Most schools do not allow such terms and have strong consequences for such homophobia, yet the dominant culture prevails. With the Obama administration and the Supreme Court recognizing gay marriage and considering the value of love over prejudice, there are now even songs on pop radio portraying homosexuality in a more positive light. Yet, most kids still snicker, many adults still judge, and never mind the hip-hop and dancehall reggae cultures, which continue to reflect the relatively dark ages of homophobia.

I made it a practice that whenever new kids came to my class, I would ask what school they went to previously and why they left it. The responses ran the gamut but generally fell into categories of disliking specific teachers, groups of other students, or administrative structures. However, one student, Caleb, told me and the entire math class that a kid had threatened to slit his throat because he was gay. I was so impressed that this young man had the cojones to come out in front of a room full of strangers on his first day in a new school. I was simultaneously depressed that such violent prejudice is still so prevalent. Even the tallest, toughest, leather-wearing homosexual tended to stay closeted. The rest of the kids were silent because although there were some very limp-wristed, high-voiced, makeup-wearing boys at our school, none would openly admit to being gay, even after being elected class president, like Caleb did.

Obama opened the floodgates on gay rights with his second-term inauguration speech, but until then it was "don't ask, don't tell" in the military, marriages, and courtrooms. Once again, my libertarian upbringing shines through, and I know from experience that I have seen some very stable homosexual couples raise some successful straight children. I know the Bible and many other religious books say a lot, but they are all admittedly patriarchal, and they can be misogynistic in their extremes. Biblical literalists and Torah scholars must have an equally hard time with all the covenants regarding tattoos, divorce, diet, and judgment of others.

I do not want to come off as antireligious, because I love parts of every holy book I have read, even the golden tablets of the Latter Day Saints. Many such books have also been used to justify male dominance, racism, slavery, war, and genocide. I just refuse to believe that any God would choose sides in a war, like some Greek tragedy, Hindu myth, or Book of Revelation. I believe that we must each have an individual relationship with the Spirit, in whatever form it speaks to us, and that actions speak louder than words. I really hope my children grow up in a world where people do not consider "gay" derogatory, and where they are measured by the content of their character.

I used to believe so much in free will that any biological determinism was beyond my comprehension, but the more I teach and the older my kids get, the more I realize we are each dealt a deck of cards in life. Call it karma, call it genetics, or call it fate, children's temperaments and tendencies are seen so early on that it is actually scary. I still believe that family, culture, and choice can mitigate almost any biological tendency, but being gay is not something that needs fixing.

Now we are moving into the era of transgender children and it poses real questions about gender identity, sports, bathrooms and locker rooms, and equality. I used to be so liberal that I thought we should do away with gender specific bathrooms like we got rid of segregated water fountains. I have since tempered my hopes for total equality, but as teachers we are supposed to treat boys and girls equally. Yet being a male teacher does require a different rapport with each gender, especially in middle school.

31

Mosquito-Bite Phobia

We are better off when women are empowered—it leads to a better society.

John Legend

Male teachers receive special training in how to avoid a sexual harassment accusation: never be in a room alone with a student, never touch a female student, never give a student a ride home, and never ask about her boyfriend, sex life, or choice of fashion. Of course, this does not stop girls from flirting with teachers, and some even seem to take sick pride in flaunting their role as temptress. Katie was always trying to talk about sex, her boobs, and her boyfriend in math class, and although I have a discipline system, she rode the razor line with dangerous proximity.

When I had a discussion about middle-school girls' statistical drop in math and science scores compared to earlier years and encouraged my homeroom girls to not get sucked into the hype of body image over substance, she countered with, "Guys do not care if I am good in math; they care about my boobs." Of course, I nipped it in the figurative bud, but I was shocked at her forthright assessment of what mattered to her and her peers.

The next day as I was helping her neighbor with graphing equations, she lowered her shirt and bra to "show her friend her mosquito bite." Unfortunately, I looked over just in time to glance at her half-exposed breast. I immediately stared at the ceiling and blurted, "Whoa, Katie, please pull your shirt up—that is totally inappropriate for class." But only a blind man would have missed my obvious embarrassment. I turned red, kept my stare 180 degrees away until the coast was clear, and then told her if she did that again she'd be going home. Of course, she did not do it again, but you could just see her impish smile of contentment at having completely flustered her male teacher.

I obviously still have some sexism because I would have kicked a guy out immediately for showing part of his genitalia. As much as I try to avoid it, I still treat guys and girls differently in class. I have taken workshops, trainings, and I try to be a self-reflective teacher, so I think admitting my sexism is the first step. I like it when girls are intellectually assertive in class, and I do not let guys dominate or objectify women.

Most schools now have dress codes regarding male "sagging" pants and female cleavage, belly buttons, and lengths of skirts. Despite this, kids often push the boundaries, and we kept a special tub of extra clothes for violators. I quickly learned that a male teacher could not tell a female student that her breasts were showing or her skirt was too short. Even when I would request a female teacher to confront the violation, a few of the defiant teens would still say, "It's not my fault he was looking at my breasts." If a student violator entered my classroom, even if I immediately got a female teacher to get them an oversized baggy T-shirt, I had to be ready to be accused of looking at her breasts.

These types of behaviors are obvious cries for male attention, but in the unhealthiest ways imaginable. Some of these girls would prefer a fat, hairy forty-year-old hitting on them, as it sadly reminded them of their sexually abusive fathers, uncles, and other scumbags from whom they have gotten some approval and attention. It is like the daughter of an alcoholic abuser marrying her worst nightmare, and thus continuing the cycle of family abuse. I tried to understand and break the chain, but when I saw them choose the meanest boy in school as a boyfriend, it was all I could do not to tell them they could do much better. Of course, despite my best intentions, advising young women on their dating choices would be totally inappropriate and an invitation for a sexual harassment lawsuit.

My close friend teaches middle-school social studies, and after he moved two girls into separate homerooms, one of them accused him of sexual abuse to get out of his class. This is devastating in any profession, but in teaching it can be the end of a career, even if one is found innocent. The teacher was a total family man with several children, he had no prior record or suspicious behavior, and there was no evidence against him other than the student's word. Unfortunately, as it turns out in this case, any accusation must be investigated and the teacher put on administrative leave until cleared of all claims. This would not only deeply affect his class, curriculum, reputation, and family but would also be personally devastating after dedicating his life to serving children.

Despite contrary advice from his union lawyer, his supervisor, and his principal, this brave young teacher called up the accuser's mother and explained the homeroom switch situation. He offered to meet with them in person, introduce his family, explain his side of the story, and give the girl a chance to confront him and tell her truth. Of course, when she was facing this route instead of lawyers, mediators, and counselors, she broke down and admitted the whole ploy. I still cannot believe he actually made that phone call, but I have to admire his dedication to truth and integrity, and thank his lucky stars that they did not sue him for harassment just for calling. When lawyers run the world, we descend into a world of liability.

We live in a very litigious society, and I have seen threats of lawsuits change district policies many times. Some teachers joke that a superintendent's main jobs are to avoid lawsuits and say no. In one case, I was subtly threatened with a lawsuit after a homeschooled boy joined our program and used a blindfolded trust game as a ploy to walk an older girl into a concrete pit.

Instead of apologizing for his son's outrageous cruelty, the young boy's dad said, "I would be more careful doing games where kids can get hurt like that. You could get sued." This father also once told me to "be careful how you talk to my wife" after I told her that she needed to speak to the principal about grade-placement issues. He was also known to uncomfortably corner female teachers at the gym, and frequently used intimidation as a way to manipulate the system. Of course, teachers are not the only people to suffer from sexual harassment and litigious helicopter parents, but I think we take the brunt. It is easy to let these threats take the wind from one's sails, but I still prefer to ask for forgiveness rather than permission.

I have taken some crazy risks as a teacher—leading all manner of activities: nonbiker kids on mountain bike rides, blind kids on ropes courses, out-of-control, first-time sledding in the backcountry, backwoods capture-the-flag games with rusty barbwire fences, rattlesnake and scorpion wrangling, aboriginal fire starting, obsidian flint knapping, bike-path wildcrafting, dollar-store runs for ponchos in October downpours, and nighttime hikes without flashlights. These memories make for thrilling stories, but none of them scared me as much as that teenager's mosquito bite.

32

OVERMEDICATED YOUTH

It is possible in medicine, even when you intend to do good,
to do harm instead. That is why science thrives on actively
encouraging criticism rather than stifling it.

Richard Dawkins

There are students at almost every school who are on drugs for ADHD (attention-deficit hyperactivity disorder), OCD (obsessive-compulsive disorder), ODD (oppositional defiant disorder), MPD (multiple personality disorder), and every other acronym you could think of. My master's in special education made me sensitive to their needs, and yet my philosophical and educational background also taught me that many chemical imbalances can be changed through diet, lifestyle, exercise, and even intentional changes in attitude through prayer, meditation, and relaxation training.

My thesis, "Self-Relaxation Training for Attention-Deficit Hyperactivity Disorder (ADHD)," composed in 1995, was not well received, as it flew in the face of conventional psychiatric approaches to the disorder. In many inner-city schools, one out of four students is on Ritalin, or speed for kids. I am not totally dogmatic about my aversion to medicating children, because I have seen parents that have tried every behavioral, diet, and lifestyle approach. I even met a family that, after trying all the unconventional methods known, moved to eastern

Oregon to avoid allergens, but still found Ritalin to be most effective. After his first medication, their son turned to them and said, "For the first time, I feel like I can sit and read a whole chapter and actually remember what I read without being distracted by the sound of rain on the rooftop." Who am I to tell them they are wrong after trying everything, when their son finally feels like himself and can control his mind?

Other kids feel they lose an important part of themselves once medicated, never mind the side effects of stunted growth, addiction, and selling their drugs to others. Several students at charter school admitted to hearing voices and seeing strange beings when they were not medicated. One student had inner battles with demon voices, telling him to do bad things when he was not on medication. Of course, his dad was a jailed drug addict, and his mom a raging alcoholic, so to tease apart the influencing factors is impossible. But from a purely pragmatic perspective, I'd probably try medication, too, if I were hearing evil devils taunting me to hurt people.

Greg described forgetting to take his medication over the weekend, and out of the corner of his eye seeing a dark figure, who would disappear whenever Greg turned his head. Greg could not read, draw, watch TV, or even close his eyes to escape the lurking, menacing figure, and he could not confront him directly. So medication was the lesser of all evils. He may not have had the same depth of feelings, the emotional highs and lows, that came with his diagnosed depression and schizophrenia, but at least now he could attend school regularly and relate to other kids. The last trimester, when his mom could not afford the correct dosage, he missed several weeks in a row just lying in bed, unable to muster the strength and desire to face his demons.

When my hippie friends bemoan the overmedication of our children, I have so many stories to tell on both sides of the coin that I encourage them to avoid extremism in their supposed "liberal" beliefs. Until one has personally experienced a real chemical imbalance, one cannot judge another's experience with any validity. Even having experienced such challenges, it still doesn't give one the right to tell others not to take a pill making the difference between near-sanity and months in bed, dropping out of school, an inability to connect to others, and daily battles against oft-times invisible devils.

Upon researching ADHD for my thesis, I realized I had many of the symptoms. Since it is a behavioral disorder, undiagnosable through medical means beyond questionnaires, behavioral checklists, and anecdotal evidence, no one can say for sure who has it and who does not. In my case, I am better at multitasking than doing one thing at a time, and feel more "normal" when I am busy. My mind races constantly, I overanalyze everything, and I can be incredibly impulsive to the point of embarrassment.

Many ADHD kids of my generation just self-medicated with marijuana, but the irony is that Ritalin is actually a stimulant. Psychiatrists theorize that someone's brain with ADHD responding to a stimulant says, "Geez, I guess I am on overdrive and better slow down." When a younger, non-ADHD kid takes Ritalin, the drug has the normal stimulant effect, thus causing hyperactivity and restlessness, yet it remains the NoDoz and coffee of the current college set. It is a major black-market drug on many campuses, with kids selling them like joints and using them to cram for tests or pull all-nighters finishing papers. I am so glad I never resorted to such dangerous pharmaceutical habits.

Of course, both the drug industry and the bureaucrats would much rather medicate than address the core issues of class size, multimodal learning styles, counselor layoffs, and the withering of art, music, and PE from their curricula. It is much cheaper to pop a pill than address the underlying issues. I learned a lot at my first IEP (special ed) meeting, where the Medford School District told me they removed the need for counseling from a kid's IEP when they had to lay off his counselor because of budgetary shortfalls. I told them the student was abusive to other kids, defiant to adults, and physically threatening to his mother. They agreed "off the record" that he needed counseling, but in true bureaucratic form, they changed the paperwork to meet the budgetary constraints, rather than changing the budgets to meet the true needs of the kids.

My thesis research also taught me that paying attention is a learned behavior, reinforced through parental attention. Brain research has shown that the frontal lobe synapses are strengthened through engaging children in extended focus activities. This could be reading to your kids for thirty minutes every night, doing prolonged art activities, extended scientific observations and experiments, or anything that helps them remain focused for longer periods. Memory and attention span are like muscles that need training. As any attentive parent knows, young children are easily distracted and must be taught to stay on task. It becomes far too easy just to stick kids in front of a screen, thereby gaining some parental free time, but this only reinforces their inability to work independently.

This is the oxymoronic irony of educational video games for younger students. If a parent models playing piano for thirty minutes, reading the whole newspaper, working on a craft project, or simply sitting still and meditating, children not only see how to do it, but learn that adults find value in such activities. If the longest activity a child sees parents do is watch TV or surf the Internet, the child will follow suit.

When I watch modern cartoons, especially anime and manga, I feel downright epileptic. Some cartoons and video games even appear with a disclaimer warning, after hundreds of cases of actual epileptic seizures induced by rapid-fire images. My own children beg for more screen time, the latest touchscreen, and devices galore, but I tell them that they or their wives will thank me one day when they can play an instrument, speak a foreign language, or simply hold a human conversation without being distracted by their buzzing phones. Overstimulated lives lead to overmedicated youth, and going against society's norm requires imaginative dedication to amorphous ideals.

I now see kindergarteners using electronic tablets and iPads instead of colored pencils and paper. I see teachers using SMART boards and videos of the letter *M* bouncing across a screen instead of a blackboard. I am totally in favor of using technology whenever it provides a better way to present information, but we have to consider the long-term impact of presenting information in such visually stimulating and rapidly changing formats.

I see elementary school kids who cannot use a pair of scissors, but can cut and paste on a computer without any help. This cannot be in their long-term best interest. They may pass a test earlier in their chronology or acquire reading skills faster, but neither means that, developmentally, this type of learning represents best practices. Young children need to be learning through multimodal, often kinesthetic, methods. I can tell an engaging, educational story for forty-five minutes, commanding an entire classroom's rapt attention, and the neuronal connections formed will encourage attention span and focus for years to come. I admit I still love to show YouTube videos of time-lapse science concepts, but nothing beats experiential learning and an eloquent book.

33

THE ONLY LIBRARIES ARE IN JAILS

When I read about the way in which library funds are being cut and cut, I can only think that American society has found one more way to destroy itself.

Isaac Asimov

Many southern Oregon counties were forced to close all their new libraries because of budgetary constraints, despite brand-new, million-dollar facilities in downtown Medford, Ashland, and Talent. The voters rejected a new property tax levy, amid antigovernment political advertising, and tight purse strings superseded their children's best interests. A few local bonds have reopened them for minimal hours, but some even argued that in the age of the ubiquitous Internet, libraries were obsolete. At least we had a brand-new juvenile detention facility with a full library, so if children got arrested, they could check out a decent book.

There is always money for more jails, more wars, and more roads, but never enough for schools, libraries, and health care for the poor. It is so Shakespearean as to border on tragic comedy. I literally could not have written a better Orwellian twist than having several one-year-old, state-of-the-art libraries sitting locked and empty while meth labs and jails sprout like invasive weeds throughout our communities.

I know money will not solve all of education's problems, and I know that many people do not consider libraries necessities, but I also know that the richest country in the world could have different priorities. I will not get started on the money wasted on overseas wars, subsidies, and the military-industrial complex. I do know that Americans hold dearly to antitax views such that they had a revolution over it, and that it is still a touchy topic even today. We Americans live in a very individualistic culture, especially when compared to the family-centeredness characteristic of Asian and Arabic cultures.

Asian cultures used to value filial piety, or the belief that the elder was the center of the family. Our youth-obsessed culture has put children at the center of the family, as adults frantically cling to their wrinkle creams, gray-hair cover-ups, and surgical procedures to maintain the illusion of youth. Children are often served first at the dinner table, with grandparents cordoned off into retirement homes with little connection to the inclusive, multigenerational approach of our ancestors.

The irony is that we are not exactly preparing a bright environmental future for our children, despite our attempts to give them everything they want. Our obsession with material pleasure and accumulation of assets is the actual cause of our children's endangered future. If we did not prioritize wars for cheap oil, gas-guzzling SUVs with lone drivers, and cheap plastic disposables, we could actually create a sustainable future for our children and most of the world too.

Combine this lifestyle with Tea Party rhetoric, and we can quickly forsake our fellow humans for the sake of principle. The impact of this kind of individualism in China and India, for example, could lead to massive, American-style overconsumption of already sparse resources. On the other hand, our focus on the individual has also brought us our Bill of Rights, many freedoms, the land of opportunity, and the birthplace of unions. We simply need to balance our personal desires with the needs of future generations and remember that any society worth its weight in gold must include public libraries that are not just in jails. The state of the public library is a reflection of the health of the state.

34

I Feel Sick

Much of your pain is the bitter potion by which the physician within you heals your sick self.

Kahlil Gibran

One of the daily judgments a teacher is forced to make is whether a kid is really sick or just faking it. I have kept a kid at school who I thought was exaggerating, and learned she was admitted to the emergency room the next day for strep throat. I have also sent many students home who, I knew, happened to get sick the same day as three of their best friends, but their parents excused the absence anyway. I was amazed that some of these kids were ever well, considering their lifestyles.

I often think of my friends' dietary restrictions for their kids, from gluten-free to non-GMO and organic, and the homeopathic tinctures and supplements they take, and I am amazed what different worlds we live in. Most inner-city and trailer kids have never even heard of kale. They drink more soda than water, and they eat more processed food than fresh produce. Empty calories are better than nothing.

Jessica came to me one day saying she felt sick and needed to go home, while in one hand was a Coke and in the other a bag of sour gummy worms. As it was lunchtime, I asked her whether she had drank enough water and gotten a proper meal for lunch. She replied that Coke and gummy worms were all she had that day. "I do not eat breakfast," she said. I recommended she drink several glasses of water, get some Ramen from the cupboard, and eat something real, then see if she still felt sick later. This school invested in Top Ramen for just such common ailments. She made it through the day, but I still feel sick when I think about her lunch. It makes a school lunch of hamburger, fries, and chocolate milk sound nutritious. Compared to gummy worms, ketchup is probably a vegetable, as Bush Sr. once asserted in his school lunch nutrition requirements.

I worked for a decade at an amazing after-school and summer program in Medford called Kids Unlimited, and many of the students involved ate three meals a day at school. Their parents had to drop them off by 7:30 a.m. and could not pick them up until 6:00 p.m., so the federal government, local school district, and nonprofit organizations ran programs to feed them, help with homework, and run enrichment activities. The three meals provided were pretty scary looking to me, reminding me of the green hot dogs we ate in elementary school, or the deep-fried burritos of high school. Compared to no breakfast, an empty house, hanging out on the street, or worse, I have never been so proud of government cheese.

I have been part of a nonprofit trying to bring more local fresh produce to school lunches, but the obstacles are daunting. Most school lunch programs are run by Sodexo, a multinational corporation that makes decisions which are very hard to change. The federal government definitely makes standards that preclude a lot of local produce, focusing instead on cheaper, factory-farmed sources. There are many examples of schools and communities that have made significant improvements, such as famous author and chef Alice Waters' collaboration with the Oakland School District. The impetus for change must come from the parents and students too.

Our nonprofit worked with a local director of food services who fed over 1,000 kids a day, yet had never used a carrot peeler. They literally made almost all their meals from processed foods that came frozen in a plastic bag, or canned. When presented with one hundred and fifty pounds of local carrots for the first time in his life, he had to call our executive director to be talked through his dilemma. This man cared about children and their health, but could not afford local produce compared to the mass produced items. Only after our executive direc-tor lobbied Senator Ron Wyden to alter the National Farm Bill did we equalize a few subsidies for local organic produce and monocropped industrially processed foods. This reduced the economic barriers but getting local food in schools also requires planned crop rotation, farm-er cooperatives, distribution hubs, and a lot more time and work than ordering all your food from Sysco. Parents who do not have time to make their kid's lunch probably will not start a campaign for healthier lunches, so it is up to the community to improve the situation.

Most parents I meet are hardworking, caring, frugal, young people who are working full-time, overtime, or two minimum-wage jobs. They cannot easily call in sick, take a day off when their kid is sick, or provide consistently healthy meals. Most would prefer higher-quality school meals. We are what we eat, so we reap exponential medical savings in later life by investing in healthy eating habits as children. America is very different from England in that there is a genuine possibility of be-coming destitute, homeless, and dying on the street because of a lack of medical insurance, and it makes me sick.

35

~

MAKING HIM WANT TO BE ALIVE

Through the evolutionary process, those who are able to engage in social cooperation of various sorts do better in survival and reproduction.

Robert Nozick

Sam's grandma patted me on the back and said, "Thanks for making Sam want to be alive again." It was validating because the kid rocks back and forth on his heels and discusses quantum theory and ethics in the same breath, but he has a really hard time with his peers. Acne-faced and pockmarked, he is nonetheless a smart and nice kid; as with many students with special needs, though, he is awkward and stilted in his interactions, like an Einstein among sheep. When covering genetics in biology, he suggested genetically modifying a virus to inject medicines into diseased cells, and that night I found an article about the very same project done in labs. He was so happy to know that a teacher took enough interest in his wacky tangents to validate his theories.

I met his parents at a parent-teacher-student conference and found out that they lived in California with Sam's two half-brothers, leaving Sam to be raised by his grandparents. He was clearly excited to have his parents and grandparents at the conference such that he could barely sit still while rocking back and forth in proud gesticulations.

There are many goals of effective education, many best practices for optimum learning, but the primary underlying factor has to be some sort of value, appreciation, or—hopefully—joy of learning. So many underserved kids have become so accustomed to failure and lack of support that they learn to mask their challenges through coping mechanisms. Such misbehaviors are not an indicator of low intelligence.

I am a firm believer in rote learning, the fundamentals of math and reading, and strict discipline systems, but I also want my students to love my class. I want my class to be the part of the day that they look forward to, the teacher who can support their learning and their lives. I want to help them work harder than they ever have before and feel proud of their work. I am satisfied just to help a kid want to come to school again, but to help Sam want to be alive again was humbling. It was confirmation that I was already becoming much more than just a teacher.

On the best days, a swing on a monkey bar will make a young boy see teachers in a whole new way. He will come to my home decades later to visit with his dad, his handshake firm like his gaze. On my worst days, I seriously question my career choice and doubt my abilities to make any lasting difference. I am sometimes too easily disillusioned by the immensity of the task, but more often than not, I am continually amazed by the beauty, innocence, and sheer joy of children's imaginative worlds. I have taken kids on a field trip where the chaperone said the kids had restored her faith in humanity. Money and prestige cannot buy that feeling. I know that any sane teacher has moments when he or she wants to quit, but when my hair stands on end upon witnessing a moment of cooperation, generosity, or empathy. I remember why I chose this path. I chose the path of life, the path of inspiration, the path of changing the world through serving children, with honesty and integrity.

36

~~~~~

I Am Not a Snitch

How could you be from the ghetto and be a rat?

Suge Knight

*T*here has always been a stigma among kids against tattletales, narcs, momma's boys, teacher's pets, and in the current lingo, snitches. From rap music to T-shirt mottos, the pressure to avoid snitching is so prevalent that even cases of assault or theft go unreported to authorities. I discussed it with my middle-school homeroom kids frequently, especially after something was stolen or a fight occurred that people could have stopped. Very few at-risk kids will trust an adult, but who can blame them when we adults do not usually help the situation; we just follow our protocols and rules and leave little room for listening. Usually police just give tickets and arrest people, teachers just kick you out of classes, principals send you to detention, and parents ground you. I have been on both the giving and receiving ends of this systemic response to people's mistakes, and I know we are all trying to help, but we are stuck in a reward-and-punishment model of enticing right action. If teachers try to address a situation from outside the system and its rules, they risk their jobs and licensure.

We had at least ten iPods stolen one year, and we had no idea how to handle it beyond banning them. Student government came up with a detailed system of tracking them with serial numbers, making rules about their usage, and even warning students that further thefts would result in their ban. Nevertheless, someone stole one. I knew that several of the kids knew who did it, but they were just too afraid to tell anyone. I always hope someday I can teach them to think differently.

My own father taught me to lie to get a cheaper ticket at the movies or ski resort. My mother, on the other hand, believed that honesty was more important than money. I am glad I took my mother's advice, and that I am teaching my own children a high degree of integrity. I often tell my kids, "You know I am a man of my word, so..." I try to be mindful and consistent in my words with my own children and in the classroom. Being honest is not being a snitch, but I also respect people who handle issues directly rather than calling the police or lawyers at the drop of a hat.

I am not a snitch, but I will stand up to a bully, tell a stranger's kid not to act that way, and confront my own friends about their integrity on fishing standards, clipped ski tickets, or stealing from multinational corporations. We all justify our poor choices, and I would hope my true friends would call me out on my own false justifications as well. Some call me confrontational, but after so many years teaching children to do the right thing, it has forced me to face my own hypocrisies. I am by no means perfect. I definitely avoid paying a fine if I can, often defy laws I feel are senseless or wrong, and still try to talk my way out of mistakes with my wife. As a father and husband, I have often had to make amends, change my flawed beliefs, and accept valuable criticism. That self-reflection is what makes us human and leads to personal evolution and better teaching.

I teach kids to evaluate their effort, learning style, and ultimately the quality of their own work honestly. If such honesty is communicated to others, it requires us all to snitch, but directly to the person who is making bad choices. When a bully encounters the "bystander effect," he or she feels empowered to continue and escalate. But if just one person actively confronts the bully, verbally empathizes with the target, or reports it to an adult, the bullying behavior diminishes.

I have to hold back on this teacher instinct in situations of scolding a stranger's children in the supermarket, advising a parent I have never met about proven strategies, or just asking my wife, "Well, what did this situation teach you?" I confronted two kids at the skate park about stolen longboards and then turned the boards in to the police. A neighbor, whose mom called to thank us for returning her kid's birthday present, claimed them both. If that is being a snitch, then I will gladly wear the scarlet letter and teach kids to follow their hearts. If we each take a moment to listen, our heart knows the right thing to do. Emotional intelligence and discernment are hard to teach, but my wife's intuition has gotten us through our hardest times.

37

THE PATH LESS TRODDEN

*Breathe. Listen for my footfall in your heart. I am not gone
but merely walk within you.*

Nicholas Evans

After I lost count of the miscarriages, our second child was born eight weeks prematurely. Instead of our planned homebirth with midwives, we ended up at the big city hospital. Aside from the protocols involved in taking a shower and the monitors and nurses who said she was not having a baby until they decided to look at her 10 cm dilated cervix, the hospital's technology was just what the doctor ordered. This particular hospital did not even allow smoking on the sidewalks outside the building, so smokers had to cross the street. They also had a protocol that an expectant mother had to be on an IV and transported in a wheelchair. These two rules together, literally lead to pregnant women being pushed across streets in wheelchairs with a rolling IV bag in one hand and a cigarette in the other.

I could not help but feel angry at these women and their "friends," willing to push them across the street, while my wife ate organic collard greens and took every multivitamin she could, only to end up with our baby struggling just to survive. I give thanks that machines exist to keep babies alive, whether they are from earth mamas or smoking mothers, and that whatever justice there is in this universe is beyond my judgment.

The hospital's formula for preemie babies listed corn syrup as the first ingredient, and many of the preemies had colic, gas, reflux, and other digestive issues. We supplied our own supplement for breast milk, baby wipes, cotton blankets, and constant cuddling. I really empathized with those who settled for the overpriced bulk hospital items. To help make up for the lack of care or time from some parents, the hospital had many volunteer "cuddlers" who came in just to hold and cuddle the infants, especially skin to skin. Despite all the modern technologies, nothing seems to replicate this human element, which is statistically proven to improve outcomes.

It is amazing that, in this day and age of high-tech lifesaving devices, even Western medicine has to recognize the power of the human touch, the shared sound of a heartbeat, and the smell of a mother's skin. As the father of a premature infant, aside from supporting my wife, the only thing I could do was hold my son like he was all I had on earth. I taught him to breathe with my breath, to regulate his heart with my heartbeat, and to know he was cared for with my voice and the smell of my skin. He was intubated to help him breathe, but his heart has always been strong.

I always keep a picture of my own children in my classroom so that I can remember that each of my students is someone's angel. At one point, each of these guys was an innocent little tabula rasa, with all their genetic and family baggage beyond their control. Sometimes, when I am about to really lose it and say something biting or sarcastic to a student, I have to take a deep breath, look at the photo of my children, and remember that, for the most part, it is really not their fault. I have been so lucky, so blessed, and so privileged, yet every choice I have made has also helped to build or destroy what I have been given.

That is why we gave the middle schoolers ten chances more than the older kids because they were not as responsible for their situations and had much more hope of reform. Some eventually made lemonade, while others repeatedly squirted lemon juice in your eye. A teacher cannot take insults personally, it just widens the target.

The myelination of neurons can begin incredibly early if one is not taught to expand synaptic connections. An adult's character predictably correlates to a child's choices. A second language or a second

PlayStation—such decisions hinge on a matter of a parent's choice, not a child's.

At some point, each of us must take responsibility for our own situation and stop blaming our parents, society, or anyone else for our situation. Of course, this is different if you are a refugee in Darfur or the victim of a disease, but even then, all we really have to control is our attitude and our choices of how to handle our lot in life. As our premature baby has taught me, we take aim, and the universe takes over. We must remember to breathe deeply, do our best, and let love do the rest. Raising children is the greatest teacher training because it frees us with the strength of powerlessness. There are so many aspects of our own lives, and even our own bodies, that are totally beyond our control.

38

LATE FOR THE EMERGENCY ROOM

Care shouldn't start in the emergency room.

James Douglas

After a particularly hard day at work and despite a pounding headache, I did not take any painkillers. By the time dinner was over, the left side of my face had stopped working. I figured I was either having a heart attack or some strange nerve issue, so in typical postmodern objectification, I searched the Internet for explanations. I concluded it was either Bell's palsy, a pinched nerve, a brain tumor, or a heart attack. I did not have any of the other signs of a heart attack—numbness in the extremities, fuzzy thinking, chest pains, or blurred vision—so I concluded I should just try to sleep it off. I said my prayers and tried to go to sleep, except my eye would not shut, so I had to put an eye pillow on it to keep it closed all night.

Upon awakening to the same issue, I called my doctor, who said I should have gone to the emergency room the night before. I quickly tried to scribble some substitute plans, print them, and run the materials to school before I went to the emergency room. I was in such a rush to get there and gone that a police officer pulled me over for speeding. I tried to explain why half my face wasn't working but broke down in tears, hoping he'd just let me go. He said, "Well, if you think you might be having a heart attack, I can't just let you drive off, so I have to call the ambulance to check you out." Thirty minutes later, a full checkup by the paramedics confirmed my Internet diagnosis of Bell's palsy, but the doctor still recommended I head straight to the hospital just to have some more tests done. They gave me a clean bill of health to drive, the officer gave me the speeding ticket, I delivered my substitute plans on time, and I finally made it to the hospital. I kept that ticket as a reminder of my workaholism.

I am by no means suggesting that any sane person, a teacher or not, should pursue this level of martyrdom, but I honestly could not imagine my principal or emergency substitute having to make do with no substitute plans. This mix of self-importance, thinking the world needs me so badly, and self-sacrifice, thinking I must always serve others first, is perhaps what makes such dedicated teachers. I know so many teachers who spend so many hours beyond their contract, use vacation time to research new lesson ideas, and come in on crutches or with laryngitis.

As I sat in the waiting room of the ER, I wrote my final words to my children and wife as I strongly considered my mortality. Perhaps I am just melodramatic, but my doctor and the paramedic could not rule out a heart attack, and losing control of one's face is a little disconcerting. Many tests later, they also concluded I had Bell's palsy, an inflammation of the cranial nerve for which Western medicine cannot claim causation. While more prevalent in pregnant women, it usually just goes away in three weeks to three months, though it can leave deadened nerves and partial facial paralysis, a crooked smile, or a droopy eye. I tried acupuncture, massage, anti-inflammatories, ice, relaxation, and a change of perspective that the whole substitute-plans, speeding-ticket fiasco made so obviously necessary. I had been running around from 6:00 a.m. to 10:00 p.m., working for everyone else and not taking care of myself. I was also letting daily stresses affect me too much and forgetting what was truly important—my family, my health, and my attitude.

I took a couple of days off, then went back to work with half a face working. It was quite a challenging experience, with one eye that would not shut or squint in the sun, a lip that would not blow the whistle or sing our morning songs, and a face that was exhausted at the end of the day. Of course, I had to be careful eating and drinking, but the most interesting aspects were more about blinking, resting my eyes, sunlight, and the humbling experience of explaining that I could not blame the dentist for my partial paralysis. I did a much better job of sitting down for breakfast, resting at my lunch break, getting home at a decent hour, taking time to relax and unwind, and stopping work at home past 8:00 p.m. I no longer returned kids' work the next day or wrote as many comments on papers, but the result was I was much less stressed. The kids, other faculty, and parents were so supportive that I really felt loved. I asked for a lot more help, which was something I learned the hard way. I still have not learned how to say no, but I try not to be late for the emergency room.

39

~

SITTING DOWN TO PEE

The most precious gift that marriage gave me was the constant impact of something very close and intimate, yet all the time unmistakably other, resistant—in a word, real.

C. S. Lewis

Someone once advised me never to teach at my neighborhood school unless I did not mind seeing kids I know everywhere I go. I spent most of my teaching career living in a small liberal town in southern Oregon, where we were famous for not immunizing our kids and, until recently, allowing public nudity. I have never had a teaching job in this university town, where student teaching is the golden ticket. I did, however, see some parental and spousal decision making that made me think I was in a television sitcom.

We lived in the kind of town where men's groups played drums around the fire circle and men negotiated and got permission for the privilege of watching sports on TV at home. I have always been proud to be a humanist and do not believe a man should rule the home, or even be the head of the house like the Bible says. I appreciate a woman's right to work, reproductive choice, and equality of opportunities, yet have seen certain issues taken too far by some of my friends' wives. For example, when his young boys were learning to pee on their own, Richard's wife said they should learn to pee sitting down so they did not make such a mess. Richard was fine with the boys sitting down to pee, but his wife then told him that his boys would only do what their daddy did, so he needed to start peeing sitting down as well. Talk about the ultimate emasculation—not just telling a man that he should pee sitting down, but arguing angrily at a multifamily gathering to prove her point. Do not get me wrong; I love a fiery woman, and this one gave birth at home without a midwife, so she can walk the talk. I was just glad Richard knew how to say, "Yes, honey," while still standing up for his right to pee standing up.

This has been, I think, the key to a happy marriage with a fiery, assertive woman. The cliché was "happy wife, happy life," but I said, "Choose your battles, and avoid the wars." After we had kids, we all knew we could not just go snowboard whenever we wanted, but we also established the annual guys' snowboarding-weekend trip. We still made time for fishing, biking, boating, and other "guy time," while prioritizing our kids' and wives' needs. We need date nights, weekends away from kids, check-ins, and calm, honest communication to make our marriages work. We have also all learned to bite our tongues, tuck our balls between our legs, and mumble under our breath like disgruntled clerks.

Selective hearing and low-tone grumbling are just the price we have paid to have intelligent, independent, assertive wives. We live in a society that values blond bimbo babes for their external "assets," but who would really want to live with a ditsy, submissive, dependent woman? Well, sometimes even I can dream of a fantasy cheerleader, but I know in my heart I prefer a career leader. I have raised my children to value a woman's worth based on her character, not her shape. I know that if women had more political and economic power, we would have a more balanced world. This has been inherent in my focus on math and science for middle-school girls, who tend to lose their early academic advantage over boys during these crucial adolescent years. They start to focus more on being attractive than smart.

As much as I have wanted to believe in total gender equality, I have seen such stark gender differences at such young ages that reality has not confirmed my idealistic hopes. I still believe that many gender differences are simply overlapping bell curves with a lot of hairy women and high-voiced men. While the average man can bench press more than the average woman, there are many women who can bench more than that average guy. Since women overlap men in so many areas and we tend to focus on the averages, not the outliers, gender stereotypes remain. I cannot deny the averages, but I also cannot deny the individual potential of each person to defy those averages.

I have seen parents try to force the gender differences out of their children, only to have their son join the special forces division of the marines. My boys loved to play dress-up way past when most would find it embarrassing, but I have always encouraged the breakdown of gender stereotypes. They still loved slingshots and Nerf guns but were sensitive enough to knit, draw, and craft. They still loved to skateboard and bike, but they had to be taught to sit down and practice ukulele or memorize times tables. It has never been a question of nurture versus nature to me, since the nature part is beyond our control. The only part we can change is the nurture, so we might as well do as much as possible to bring more balance to our world. Even though phylogeny does not recapitulate phytogeny, we have some real animal tendencies to contend with.

They say that a newborn recognizes its mother's voice within the first few minutes of being born, since it sucks at a faster rate than when listening to a stranger's voice. If a father reads to his baby momma's belly every night, that baby will come out knowing its father's voice too. No matter how hard we try to prove what is natural, we can only judge by the fruits of our actions. One parenting book says use attachment parenting, another recommends love and logic, and my parents used Dr. Spock to answer any question. Now, I see kids who tell their parents what to make for dinner, how they want their eggs, and when their parents can have a date night. Our family, with two teachers as parents, is even guilty of deferring too much power to our children, but in this town, we have parents whose four-year-olds ask for breast milk, whose five-year-olds cannot sleep in their own beds, and whose six-year-olds are deciding whether they feel like going to school today.

I am in no place to judge, since I thought countless studies had proven the authoritative parenting style best. Then I had a second child, who called my bluff during a two-hour time-out at age three. He refused to say sorry even after two hours, and I obviously had to change my one-size-fits-all parenting style. I cannot say that there is one best parenting style for all kids in all situations, but I can say that in all my years of teaching, the kids with the most active, involved, and loving parents do the best. You could be Richie Rich or Fat Albert, thick as a brick, or bright as a light; a parent's choices in the first decade of life will last their children a lifetime. The same applies to marriage styles. You could be swingers, fundamentalists, or sleep in separate beds; as long as there is love, commitment, and honest communication, it really does not matter if you pee standing up.

40

BODILY FLUIDS

Real men change diapers!

Nick Cannon

As a father, I have finally gotten used to being peed on, pooped on, and expeditiously avoiding being puked on. As a teacher, I have also handled bodily fluids that I hope my two boys never excrete. I am sure that worse stories abound, like the time my mom caught my first son's poop in her hand so it would not land on the carpet. But here are just a handful to prepare teachers for their chosen profession.

One of the programs I worked for shared space with the local Boys & Girls Club, who came in right at 3:00 after my students had left at 2:30. Of course, this was a hard transition for a teacher who liked to stay late and get ahead, because after-school programs are not known for being calm and quiet. It did not help that the club also needed to have a pool table and two foosball tables in my classroom as part of the sharing agreement. Many mornings, we would return to messy classrooms and missing or misplaced property, but we were very surprised when the boys' bathroom seemed to still smell like poop in the morning. Of course, boys are stinky, and so is poop, but for it to still smell so strongly in the morning was odd. This smell continued for a week, despite my asking the custodian to investigate the situation. He found nothing out of the ordinary until a week later, when he decided to give the toilet a plunge to see if that helped relieve the off-gassing. Lo and behold, what do you suppose he found right under the plunger? A stale old turd! In his twenty years cleaning up after children's defecation, our custodian had never seen someone miss the toilet by this far. We laughed with dropped jaws and concluded it must have been intentional.

We approached the Boys & Girls Club coordinator, and asked her to keep a closer eye on after-school boys' bathroom usage and try to catch the offender in the offensive position. It happened two more times, without the culprit being caught, but the third time he was caught with his pants down, and he was a third-grade student. This poor child came from a very abusive and negligent home, and we could only conclude it was a painful cry for attention. These types of intentional fecal vandalism are a sure sign of a severely dysfunctional home life, and something that most people would never assume a teacher would have to face. This was someone's pride and joy, someone's blessed baby, someone that a teacher had to try to educate every day, and I can only guess at the pain hidden behind the stony demeanor. Of course, this one cried out—how many more are there who never let it show in any form, and who are held to the same state standard as a wealthy, stable family's child? Testing will not help this child, but a thorough education can break the cycle of violence that led him to this sad fate.

On the other end of the spectrum was the common occurrence in middle school of a girl getting her first period. It was so strange to see these little sixth-grade children turning into pubescent adolescents right before my eyes, but I never got used to a student coming up and whispering, "I need to go see the nurse." When I would ask why, they often had a euphemism at hand, but often they would just say, "I got my period and don't have anything." Usually, however, they would send a friend up to ask for them because they were so embarrassed. Having two boys, I never knew what to say except "go ahead" and try not to turn red. I have even had to tell a girl that she had blood on her pants and hope the office staff had an extra pair. This only goes to show that such a powerful moment is often entrusted to the hands of a teacher, to honor and tactfully help.

The other bodily fluids of urine in the bathroom, blood on the playground, and mucus running down the face are just common procedure for teachers, and we barely bat an eye. While I have become a master of urinary tract risk by holding my own pee for hours on end, I have been in many situations where there is no staff bathroom at all, thus forcing teachers to pee next to students. In some schools, the bathroom floors were so wet that I could only assume that a student actually peed directly on the floor. On those days, contrary to customary habit, I took my shoes off outside my house.

The most difficult bodily evacuation for me to handle, as a teacher and a parent, has got to be vomit. I do not even want to describe it, because it is one of my phobias, and given my slight hypochondria, it makes me even more afraid to get near enough to smell it for fear of attracting its contagion. However, one cannot call oneself a master teacher unless one has dealt firsthand with puke. I will spare the details, but some kids have breath control, and others do not even seem to know it is coming at all. Some require no help or cleanup, while others a full change of clothes and their neighbor's clothes also.

I still have not gotten used to this aspect of teaching, and whether on long bus rides, overnight field trips, or after a perfect execution in the toilet, I always try to defer to custodians, fellow teachers, or even parent volunteers. We concoct a strange brew in the hydrochloric acid of a classroom, and few people with master's degrees so often face this potent equalizer of men and boys alike. Being a teacher is such a humbling experience, sharing the highs and lows, the joys and frustrations, the successes and mistakes of each child with such love. I will always seek the beauty in the crustiest nose, the stinkiest boys, and the deepest fears within others and myself.

41

BLADDER-CONTROL CONFERENCES

We are born amid feces and urine.

St. Augustine

*T*eaching programs rarely warn prospective teachers about the increased risk of urinary tract infections because of the paucity of opportunities to relieve bladder pressure. While I always took a last-minute preventative pee before kids entered the classroom, because of mass quantities of tea, I always felt the urge to splurge before the usual break three hours later. Most people with regular jobs do not realize it is illegal to leave the students unattended even for the duration of urination; hence, most teachers control their bladders like an emcee on the mic.

Timing, rhythm, volume, and, of course, spontaneous flow at the drop of a hat make the subtle arts of teaching much like a freestyle lyrical session. While three hours is a normal exhibition of these powers, during parent-teacher conferences, this mystical art can extend to four or five hours. Trying to get through all the conferences in two days often required me to schedule back-to-back conferences from 7:30 to 12:30, take thirty minutes to perform bodily functions, then continue for another five-hour stretch. When my wife got her first kindergarten teaching position, this aspect of the conferences was her visceral memory. Especially when parents ran late or went longer than scheduled, the impossibility of taking five minutes away from the next parents forced full retention.

Parent-teacher conferences are best when they involve the students showing off their work and taking pride in their growth. I used to get really stressed about providing data, suggesting improvements, and answering questions until a master teacher told me, "The parents are just as nervous as you and really just want to feel good about their child." With that mantra in mind, I heartily changed my attitude toward conferences. I began seeing them as a celebration of the child's learning rather than a chance to document and fix their academic problems. I preferred phone calls, after-school conferences, e-mails, notes home, and other structures for improving study habits, and parent-teacher conferences worked best for me when the student did not cry. I have had plenty of parents cry with pride, but fewer and fewer kids cry with shame. Some children got so nervous, they had tears welling up before we even started, and each needed a different degree of prodding and coddling to narrowly avert a meltdown.

Some of the strangest parent-teacher conferences involved the dynamic between parents, with the classic divorced parents requesting separate conferences. Many could attend the same conference despite divorce, but most requested separate conferences, especially if both had remarried. Some parents brought all their kids, and we would discuss one child while the others tugged on the mom's pants or put class tools in their mouths. I learned to provide a box of quiet toys and books just in case, but I never got used to parents parenting their kids while doing a conference. Some parents could totally ignore the toddler with a Popsicle on the piano, but I had to clarify which box was for them to play with. I was always so grateful that single moms with multiple toddlers even showed up for a conference that I always tried to accommodate.

Another aspect of teaching, rarely discussed, is the close, deep interpersonal bonds and insights into people's personal lives that teachers are afforded. I have been asked to mediate in couples' disagreements over parenting issues, seen wives break down in tears over their husbands' behaviors or attitudes, and heard fathers complain about "his mother" being to blame for all that is wrong with a child. The first time a parent broke down, I gave advice, but eventually I just learned to listen and give tissues instead. If they asked for suggestions, I was glad to provide them, but when it came to marital advice, I only gave them the same nonviolent communication skills I taught their kids: express your feelings with "I" statements, and ask for what you need in a calm, respectful way. Even with kids, that does not always work, but adults seem to make everything even more complicated.

I would often try to find the synthesis between the parent who believed the child should be self-motivated and the one who wanted more structure. I would support the parent lobbying for more reading time at home but acknowledge the need for chores, outdoor exploration, and exercise. In one instance, I was asked ahead of time by the wife to discuss the effects riding to school alone was having on her fifth-grade daughter. She also asked me to discuss her husband's late nights out and the need for him to support his daughter more and be less hard on her to be independent. I actually agreed with her but found the whole situation very sticky.

I asked my peers, my administrator, and my wife, and they all said to keep things focused on the child's needs and simply ask questions and make suggestions about improved study habits that the parents could support. Of course, I still brought up the biking issue, since that affected her energy level at school, but declined to comment on the father's hard-ass attitude or late nights out.

In general, this was the basic pattern of most parent styles and disputes. One parent was usually the kind to make excuses, mollycoddle, and helicopter-parent the child to the point of suffocation. The other parent would neglect and negate their child's successes, lacking emotional and structural supports to the point where nothing is ever good enough and criticisms precede compliments. We all have these parents within us. I tend to err on the side of criticism, while my wife leans toward mollycoddling. As parents, we have to know our type and seek more balance. But at parent-teacher conferences, teachers have to respect both types and try to mollify parents' contrasting needs, while an ocean ebbs and flows within our bowels.

42

⌒

RANDOM KIDS ON THE BUS

Lots of people want to ride with you in the limo, but what you want is someone who will take the bus with you when the limo breaks down.

Oprah Winfrey

While writing this book, I was only teaching part-time and running a biodiesel company. This gave me my first chance to take my own kids to school, see their first day of kindergarten, volunteer in the class, and help organize field trips. One day while on the bus, a young man next to me said, "You look just like this teacher I had named David." I reached back through the thousands of kids I had taught over the years, often more than 150 a day, and remembered. "Mike?" How could I forget a kid I brought to my house and recorded his first song on my computer?

Mike was homeschooled until fifth grade, when he joined our environmental science program, and within one year he had fully adjusted to school. He was already academically advanced, but he lacked the social skills to fit in at first. It was interesting to see him go from tight sweatpants and showing off his math skills, to skater jeans and being distracted by girls, but he needed a gentle hand. His mother was going through a third divorce and often called on me for assistance, whether requesting letters of recommendation or free babysitting. Though it was highly inadvisable, I "babysat" Mike at my house, with my wife and kids around, and this included recording a song he had written on the piano and then adding synthesizer bass, drums, and guitar.

When I recognized him on the bus, he was a young man, with a peach-fuzz moustache, long hair, and a deep voice. He was as tall as me and had a calm self-confidence that he lacked in his preadolescence. His mother and I had a slightly awkward last communication, since I had to draw the line of doing no more favors. I said I was not comfortable continuing to babysit a teenager, and she would have to make other arrangements. I was not sure how he would remember it all, but he immediately said, "You were the best teacher I ever had." I asked him why he liked my class so much, and he replied, "You always seemed like you really cared, even when we were in trouble, and you made learning fun, even if it was hard." I told him I really appreciated being his first teacher and helping him transition to mainstream middle and high school.

He got off at the next bus stop, but in this quick five-minute interaction, I felt affirmed. I think I am a good teacher, since countless students, parents, and peers have told me this. When not teaching full-time, I feel slightly rudderless. I start to question my career choices, and have even considered going back to school to get my administrative license, PhD, or even a law degree. When I saw Mike on the bus, it reminded me how much I love teaching. Whether in one minute or over many years, you never know when you will say or do the right thing to change a kid's life. I may have been burned out by a system that starts testing and remediation in kindergarten, but I deeply appreciate the lives I have changed through heartfelt education. I will never forget all these kids who have changed my life, no matter what school they came from.

43

The Perfect System

Man, the living creature, the creating individual, is always
more important than any established style or system.

Bruce Lee

always thought I would find one school that would meet my
career needs for the rest of my life, but the longest I spent at
any one school was five years. At first, I would always blame the school,
the administration, or the funding system for my dissatisfaction, but I
have come to realize the choice has always been mine. I have certainly
never been fired, but I have left because of professional differences, personality differences, and in a couple of instances, for family priorities.

Every individual has weaknesses, every organization has faults,
and every school has a unique set of challenges. Even the little red
schoolhouse, with no principal and lots of freedom for curriculum, had
parents complaining directly to teachers when dissatisfied. The other
extreme appears when applying to teach overseas in England, where all
the kids read from the same nationwide curriculum at the same hours
of the day to maximize consistency. I no longer have any dogmatic
pedagogy of education but know that small class sizes, independent
and group work, multimodal and traditional instruction, and student
empowerment are effective in any environment. It could be Waldorf,
Montessori, environmental education, technology magnet, art charter,

or homeschool support. We so often let the perfect system be the enemy of the great, and you can guarantee that no system, no matter how perfect, will ever meet the desires of every parent. As teachers, we are more concerned with meeting the needs of each unique child.

I love the freshness of a new teaching position. I love the first few years of a new program, and I love the challenge of doing something I have never done before. Whether making paper from weeds, a science unit on weaving, or singing new songs I learned that morning, I want my teaching to be alive with fresh passion. This leads to a file cabinet full of lesson plans I may never repeat, a drawer full of technology that is outdated, and certain aboriginal skills that may not look good on my resumé, but also makes for a real Renaissance man. I am truly a jack-of-all-trades and master of none, but that is a blessing because it allows me to enjoy so many aspects of life without worrying about measurement of mastery, competition, or being stuck doing the same thing simply because I have tenure.

By not moving up the union ladder in any one district, I forever hurt my chances of establishing later security in such positions. I would rather teach in a position I love for less money than hate my job, simply counting the days until retirement because I cannot afford to lose my position on the layoff list. By union contract, the last one hired is the first fired, so while all teachers can change districts and maintain their pay scale, they lose their tenure relative to the veteran teachers in that district. Therefore, most teachers try to keep to the same district for life. I respect such teachers, especially admiring their dedication, but my life has not followed that traditional career path.

I have been very lucky in my life to have outside investments and financial stability that have given me more freedom to pursue my passions. I am always grateful for the hard work of my parents, who sent me to college, helped me buy my first car and house, and gave me a head start. Having economic advantages is not a guarantee of success, and poverty can teach a resiliency that privilege cannot. If I did not have other investments and jobs to take care of, then I would have needed that resiliency to stick to one district.

44

∿

A More Perfect Union

Join the union, girls, and together say Equal Pay for Equal Work.

Susan B. Anthony

*D*espite changing school districts, I have been part of the teachers' union for most of my entire career. I have seen several documentaries and read articles that blame the unions for most of the decline of American education. I actually think there is some accuracy to the criticisms against teachers' unions, but I have not seen them hinder student learning as much as overtesting, unfunded mandates, and underfunding in general.

At my last teaching job, we ran out of white paper and had to make all copies on colored paper for the last few months of school. Dry-erase markers were hoarded like goblin treasure, and everyone was asked to do twice as much with half as many resources. Every single teacher brings in his or her own resources—from pencils, to stickers, to instruments for the kids. This is a significant personal cost for professionals who already receive a lower salary than other people with master's degrees.

During my almost two decades in the profession, I have seen some union reps who were also effective teachers, but I have also seen quite a few embattled, bitter, resentful old-timers. I was surprised one year when we were deep into contract negotiations, and we were pulling all-nighters with mediators, that one of the teachers' reps at a union meeting insinuated that an administrator was mentally disabled. They accused the person of dishonesty, not bargaining in good faith, hiding money, making personal insults, and questioning the administrator's values toward children. I was so uncomfortable that I almost spoke up, but being low on the union totem pole made me assume this was just how these teachers talked behind closed doors. Who was I to challenge their negative assessment and personal attacks on the integrity and intelligence of their opposition? The worst part is that we would still have to work with these same principals, superintendents, parent school-board members, and other administrators after exchanging such bitter words and feelings.

In this particular conflict, the younger, newer teachers were willing to make more compromises, but the older, more experienced teachers, who had reached their salary caps, were much more interested in fighting for reduced insurance premiums and stipends for those at the top of the salary scale. Most of us younger teachers understood that the economy was in a recession, and we were lucky to have help with insurance at all, but the diehards truly believed that there was money in the budget that was being hidden by line items and accounting.

It was business as usual to balance the budget on the backs of the teachers instead of actually telling parents that we can only afford a four-day week, which is what two other districts had to do. Either way, you lost that much of your salary when you cut "contact" days, but our district loved to just take away prep days, in-service days, and parent-teacher conferences and then add a few extra unpaid days off on both ends of vacations so parents wouldn't complain. The teachers were required to teach more and more standards every year, the tests got harder and harder, the passing score increased, and the percentage of students in the school who had to pass the test to avoid failing status was approaching 100 percent. All this was required with a 10 to 20 percent cut in salary, preparation time, and teaching days. In what other industry is a passing standard set at 100 percent?

At a magnet program where I was teaching, I was asked to attend IEP meetings and sign documents as a "special education teacher," just because I had a special ed endorsement. I was certainly not their case manager, nor did I draft the IEP, but in order to avoid having to deliver services, they asked me to sign. I felt very uncomfortable, since my special ed training was over a decade old, and my job description never entailed "special education teacher." It was legally questionable, and so I questioned it.

The special ed director told me, "I used to be the full-time special ed director, but they needed a half-time principal at one of the elementary schools. When they made my special ed director position only half-time, I was asked to be the principal at the elementary school with no increase in salary, no stipend, or bonus. I still have all the same tasks as when my job was full-time director, but I have half the time to do it and the other half to be the only principal this school has. We all have to do things that are not in our job description, and we're all being asked to do more with less."

I still went to my principal and said I would be glad to deliver IEP services, attend IEP meetings, and take on extra tasks, but could not sign as "special education teacher" in good conscience. He said he would work it out, and somehow he did, as at the next meeting I was asked to sign just as "classroom teacher." These are just a few examples from countless stories of overworked, underpaid teachers, and the union cannot be blamed for them all.

I think there are ways to a more perfect union, and I do not necessarily agree with always firing the last hired first, automatic annual pay raises, and the aversion to merit pay and performance-based bonuses. Knowing American history leads to a deep respect for all the improvements that unions have brought workers, but also to a knowledge of their cronyism, protectionism, and, in the worst cases, straight mobsterism. Luckily, teachers' unions are mostly just superdedicated, opinionated, passionate protestors.

I will never forget singing union-based Christmas carols with my wife and kids while the union and administration went into another round of mediation. "Contract, Contract, Contract, Now, Fa La La La La, La La, La La" was sung while we shared hot chocolate with our principal, who stopped by to say hi between mediation rounds. He was a real pleasure to work with, and if you had to choose between an overly managerial principal and a somewhat negligent, laissez-faire approach, I'd take the hands-off approach any day. He struck a fair balance, which is not how negotiations work. You ask for twice as much as you want and hope to settle for what you really want. It feels overly adversarial, favors the old guard, and doesn't allow for the freedom of experimentation that is the root of innovation. That's why I liked the at-risk charter school model, where we were all paid a flat salary, from a first-year rookie to the twenty-year veteran. If you chose to stick with that job, you had to believe in the program.

Too many old-guard union teachers stick with jobs they hate because they could never get hired at another district at their salary level, and because they'll never get laid off until everyone else is first. They frequently repeat lessons, rarely write grants, and generally do not show up for extracurricular activities. They have seen it all come and go, been asked to bend over backward, say "thank you," and ask for another. They have faced financial cuts so many times that they are just counting the days to retirement. They can still be some of the effective teachers, though, since being personable with peers is not required to maintain academic rigor with students.

I am not ready to take on the role of creating a more perfect union, but I certainly appreciate what they have done for me and my fellow Americans. I am glad we no longer have child labor, can get overtime pay for working over forty hours, and have some awareness of toxic workplace chemicals. The unions need to be reformed, but not nearly as much as school funding needs to be prioritized over new roads, wars, and the military-industrial, insurance-pharmaceutical complex. I hope the teacher's unions expand their support for new education programs and models, including seniority pay structures.

45

DREAM JOB

Throw your dreams into space like a kite, and you do not know what it will bring back, a new life, a new friend, a new love, a new country.

Anais Nin

There are so many effective alternative programs all over Oregon. My favorite teaching job was at a small environmental science magnet program for which I was the fourth- through sixth-grade cofounding teacher. This was a parent-initiated program that focused on project-based learning, environmental science, multiage classrooms, and positive discipline. I loved the combination of these elements, which the district curriculum director and a few selfless parents had researched and found evidence of widespread success in other magnet and charter programs. They took these best practices to create an idea for a magnet program, and we two teachers were left to interpret their vision.

This was my dream job because I was able to co-create it myself from the ground up, and as one of the founding teachers, I had a lot of freedom and support to implement wild ideas. We built a cob outdoor classroom and a native plant garden, planted and cared for over one hundred trees, did field studies every Friday, sang every morning together as first- through sixth-graders, and had more parent support than we knew what to do with. Unlike middle schoolers, these kids would run up and tell me they loved me, give me hugs, describe in detail everything they ate for breakfast, and detail how their cat acted that morning. I had always seen myself as a middle-school math and science teacher, but I really got used to the long-term relationships and family feeling of upper elementary teaching. As a middle-school teacher, I would see over one hundred children a day, then a different hundred the next day, so having fewer than thirty kids all day every day felt like teaching children, not just one subject.

Having three years with a child allows relationships and authority to build, and some boys would take a whole year to establish positive rhythms. Of course, it takes a special teacher to handle three years with a kid who is a troublemaker, but it requires loving the soul of that child more than you hate the misbehaviors. I would often meditate on and pray for the kids, seeking guidance from professional peers, friends, books, and yes, a higher power. I would get ideas from dreams and wake up superexcited to face that challenging student again with a fresh perspective. Of course, not all the ideas worked, but I knew that if I had three years, I had better not give up on any kid or it would be hard on both of us. I think two years could work, but for many defiant or ADHD boys, consistent rhythms and routines are hard to establish, but once effective, are best maintained.

Project-based and inquiry-based learning is my favorite modality of instruction. Of course, we all learn in different ways: some auditorily, some visually, some kinesthetically, and some intellectually. The best teachers use all these methods, and project-based learning allows more freedom to explore all the senses and pneumonic devices available. I have never met a kid who does not learn well from songs and rhymes, and this keeps the repetition and recitation of facts much more salient. I am not some new-age liberal teacher who thinks that all learning must be fun. I actually teach kids that frustration and difficult challenge is healthy for the brain, like lifting weights for the muscles. I also give them the tools to handle academic stress, which is an inevitable part of any hardworking student's life.

While project-based learning is an intrinsic motivator, I firmly believe in testing factual knowledge acquired via pencil-and-paper tests. We did so many service projects where I was sure the kids had learned what certain terms meant, yet upon traditional testing, few could demonstrate that knowledge. Obviously, the middle path is best for all, allowing kids to flex their focused, rote-learning muscles, as well as their desire to create things, help the world, and create meaning. Jean Piaget called it constructivist, and though we do not want kids to have to reinvent the wheel, watching them create the fastest potato car helps ground the intellectual knowledge of the definition of velocity, friction, and momentum. The project approach, when done properly, allows art, science, math, and all subject areas to be seamlessly interwoven, but it also requires a lot of wheel invention by teachers.

The beauty of having all these opinionated, motivated parents behind the program was that we could call upon them for every topic under the sun. Our community came into our classroom, and our classroom went out into the community. We called it a permeable classroom, which also required saying no to a lot of creative ideas. Every trimester project ended with a demonstration of knowledge that always included a community aspect. Whether we set up a local history museum, hands-on science museum, theater performance, movie showing, assembly presentation, symposium workshop, or just presented our projects to other classrooms at the mainstream schools, we always shared our learning with others.

This permeable classroom allowed service work to build relationships with experts in many fields, and I am still amazed that elementary kids could grasp principles of permaculture design, restoration forestry, wetland remediation, green building, native plant ecology, and mycology. I did not learn about those things until I was over thirty, and many adults today have never heard of such progressive topics, even in college.

It was a hard balance, trying to meet the needs of such self-educated, self-aware parents, while the district and affiliated school still pushed monthly DIBELS (reading) testing for speed and fluency, teaching to the state test, and spending the most time and effort on test-specific teaching to the lowest achieving kids who were not passing. The school was amazing, and the entire faculty, staff, and administration cared so much but still asked questions such as, "Oh, do you actually use books over there?" Those teachers were completely dedicated to their students' learning, even if they were cynical about another special program for select students. I just tried to use my positive attitude, volunteer spirit, and classroom outreach to build bridges and overcome the initial bias against change and new programs.

The positive-discipline approach was my favorite classroom management technique because it was student-centered, empowering them to solve their problems with personal responsibility, positive language, predictable consequences, and consistent structures. Much of it centered around weekly classroom meetings where children learned to express feelings, actively listen, and solve problems. We also used it to organize student fundraisers and class celebrations, and to facilitate group decision making.

Of course, group decision making can put too many cooks in the kitchen, yet many hands make light work. Magnet programs are much more favorable to districts because they can nullify them at will. Although charter schools are often the ugly stepsister that districts try to hide in the closet, they have a certain level of freedom and independence that encourages new models. Most magnet and charter programs in southern Oregon have waiting lists of dozens of students, and families are thirsty for their precious offerings. They also tend to score higher on state standards, but this could be due to the nature of the type of family that is willing to sign up, show up, and support their students' learning, more so than in mainstream programs.

Bend, Oregon, has an innovative solution to make all elementary schools into magnet programs so that even disinterested parents who lack the time to sign up their kids get a stellar alternative program. Parents who want art focus might have to get their kids across town to a different elementary if their local school is an art magnet, but every neighborhood school has a special focus, and teachers can follow that passion instead of being stuck in a position of necessity. Most magnet programs do not have the budgetary freedom of charter schools and, thus, are not as often repulsed by districts seeking to keep a tight hold on the purse strings.

Our magnet program received statewide recognition, so it had positive district support, but I still had to write grants to get us music instruction, buses for field trips, stipends for resident experts, and materials and tools for hands-on projects. I know so many teachers who write grants, have "DonorsChoose" web pages, and solicit private

businesses for everything from shoeboxes to thousand-pound boul-
ders. Exceptional teachers bring these unseen gifts to their profession—
in addition to hours of lesson planning and correcting papers outside
of class. I was fully immersed in my dream job, but also missing my
children as usual, so I decided to take a leap of faith and opted for my
dream life instead.

46

LEAVING CHILDREN BEHIND

The true meaning of life is to plant trees, under whose shade you do not expect to sit.

Nelson Henderson

Leaving any job is a challenge, but leaving a teaching position is a particularly awkward ritual. Of course, there are the requisite promises to not be a stranger and the positive intentions to continue student and professional relationships. While I still remember almost every student's first and last name almost twenty years later, I have to say that once the job is done, most of the strong connections are severed also. I always hope I have made some lasting impact on the kids, but I rarely receive a card or e-mail after the fact, indicating a desire to stay connected. The kids, parents, and most coworkers are always glad to see me years later, but the friendly words about staying in touch are usually just polite gestures.

Of course, I can tell where a kid knows me from by how they address me. "Teacher David" is a certain elementary school, "Mr. T." is a different elementary, and "Mr. Tourzan" is usually the middle-school kids. I am frequently taken aback by kids who are excited to see me and call me by name, despite my inability to remember which school they attended. This is especially true as they get older and are hardly recognizable, but I usually just try to pretend I know them. I am much better at remembering the kids' names than the parents' names.

I left the at-risk charter school job after two years, and although I always thought I wanted to work with at-risk kids, after gray hairs, nightmares, and negative impacts on my health and family, I was seriously reconsidering. I said good-bye to certain students who had the biggest impact on me in a career spanning more than two thousand kids. Those kids are the hardest to say good-bye to because so few of them have stable male role models in their lives.

I did not even know if I wanted to teach in the mainstream system anymore as I watched it go completely broke, both literally and figuratively. Most public schools in Oregon have at least thirty-five kids in a classroom, leaky roofs, an outdated curriculum, no art or music classes or even librarians anymore, and most parents blame the overpaid teachers, a lush retirement system, and lax administration for their kids' misbehaviors. Every year, the schools must budget based on projected economic numbers and then need to cut or add funding without any stability. I do not believe in just throwing money at the problem, but anyone who actually spends time in a classroom will see the crisis of our basic infrastructure; unless, of course, you live in a rich community or send your kids to a private school, which is the goal of such a starvation diet.

47

THE OWNERSHIP SOCIETY

*The real equity issue is that there are radically unequal
allocations of funds to schools. These unequal allocations
routinely disadvantage schools in central cities and in
poor rural areas. Private school choice, as it is currently
being proposed, is a smokescreen to avoid tackling this
real equity issue.*

Linda Darling-Hammond

$\mathscr{P}$art of the outspoken Republican agenda is "the ownership
society," which, like most sound bites, is really a euphemism
for something much more insidious. While the ideas of "vouchers for
school choice," "fees for library cards," and "privatizing social security" all seem reasonable, efficient, and profitable at first glance, deeper
inquiry shows the murky waters underneath. The unspoken part of the
agenda is to completely bankrupt various public institutions in order to
reduce people's faith in government and encourage them to privatize.

Why keep a "failing" school open when one could just take one's
voucher to the Catholic school down the street? Perhaps because that is
part of the foundation of a democracy—that our public systems like education, retirement, and basic health care are not subject to the whims
of the market, to the emotional fluctuations of supply and demand, and
are quaint reminders of the separation of church and state. While the

military-industrial complex may prefer to commoditize children and elders, a democracy values and invests in them all equally according to the will of the people, not politics.

I know it sounds conspiratorial to say the government is trying to bankrupt public education, libraries, social security, Medicare, and most other social services in the hopes of profiting from their privatization. Who profited most from the privatization of military services if not the very politicians who still sit on the boards of the Bechtels and Halliburtons of this world? I know it's hard to believe that some politicians would like to privatize our libraries, but like Adam Smith before them, they are not evil. They actually believe that most welfare mothers are just lazy, that the free market really does know best, and that corporate welfare is called "trickle-down economics." I know who ends up getting trickled on. This same economic elite, among whose members I have eaten at banquets, really believe that some people are best cut out for menial, low-paid labor.

That is why the minimum wage, adjusted for inflation, is lower than fifty years ago, yet CEO-to-worker pay ratios have increased exponentially. I am not a communist who thinks everyone should earn the same wage, but I would also never claim the prophetic power to choose the next Einstein through my negligence or mercy. Every kid deserves a fighting chance to pull him or herself up from poverty.

Please do not get me started, and someone knock me off my soapbox, but the point is that the problem is much deeper than one teacher can handle. On various occasions in my career, I resolved to just teach math and science, forgetting all the joys and pains of extracurricular efforts. I am not sure I can just sit by and watch our next generation be misled while continuing to quietly subvert the dominant paradigm. I know I have changed lives, but I think now I must change the system, which in turn can change many more lives. Maybe I will become an administrator, maybe a lawyer, or a politician. Maybe after some time as a work-at-home dad and an author, I will go back as just another stranded Japanese fighter pilot, blissful in obsolescence, knowing I am just a teacher and infinitely more.

ϵ P I L O G U E

Dad's Night to Cook

All great change in America begins at the dinner table.

Ronald Reagan

Since finishing this book, I returned to teaching science at a local charter school but still make time to take my kids to school almost every day. I finished another album with my friends, summited Mount Shasta, guided my family along the Pacific Crest Trail for forty miles, and became more active in local nonprofits. My family is more relaxed, and the children really appreciate having more time with me, except when it is my night to cook. I try to teach them that homemade is always better, but my littlest one reminds me, "Not when you make it, Dad." Even after a long day with kindergarteners, my amazing wife often saves the kids from eating my college-style rice and beans. We have a very tight schedule with a chart on the wall for whose day it is to pick up the kids, cook dinner, put them to bed, or make lunches, but it seems to be working. We have not forgotten to pick up a kid yet, but almost. We still sit down for dinner every weeknight and talk.

I immersed myself in books about teaching and pedagogy, and found that many researchers affirm a more holistic approach to education. While kids' stories require no statistical proof, *How Children Succeed* by Paul Tough is a thorough analysis of the data regarding the lifelong impacts of early childhood education. Richard Louv's *Last Child in the*

Woods documents the need for more outdoor experiential learning, and Howard Gardner's *Multiple Intelligences* shows the importance of multimodal teaching. Parents can learn time-tested techniques in *Building Resilience in Children and Teens*, by Kenneth R. Ginsburg. I am not a big believer in reading too many parenting books or following the latest fads, and I try to teach all my students that their own intuition is their best guide for right and wrong.

The best parenting and teaching comes from simple things like reading and talking with your kids, being calm and respectful, and above all, from unconditional love. We all have parenting, teaching, and personal hurdles to overcome. We all have familial and cultural patterns we need to change, but deep down inside we all possess the wisdom to do the right thing. I want to thank my own parents for raising me with so much love and care. I would not be who I am without them. I also deeply appreciate my wife, who put up with me through all my ups and downs. My older brother has always been my guide.

I am so grateful to all the inspiring teachers that guided me, especially Gary Bacon from the Learning Community at Los Altos High School. His progressive methodologies and holistic pedagogy guided my views on a school's potential to change the world. I want to personally thank all the teachers, students, and especially parents who have entrusted their most cherished gifts to me. These pages are their lives, and they reflect a part of me. If these words help someone, then our stories have made the world a better place, one person at a time. To all the teachers out there, please remember, we are changing the world every day so always bring your passion and purpose to that higher calling.

www.ingramcontent.com/pod-product-compliance
Lightning Source LLC
Chambersburg PA
CBHW061729020426
42331CB00006B/1161